Don't Buy the Lie

A Book for Today's Teens

Revealing the Plots and Plans of the Enemy

Daniel S. Holmes M.Ed.

Don't Buy the LIE!

Daniel S. Holmes M. ED.

Don't Buy the Lie

ISBN: 978-1-55452-079-4
LSI Edition: 978-1-4600-0904-8

To order additional copies, visit:
www.essencebookstore.com

Guardian Books is an imprint of *Essence Publishing,* a Christian Book Publisher dedicated to furthering the work of Christ through the written word. For more information, contact:
20 Hanna Court, Belleville, Ontario, Canada K8P 5J2
Phone: 1-800-238-6376 • Fax: (613) 962-3055
Email: info@essence-publishing.com
Web site: www.essence-publishing.com

I dedicate this book to the memory
of the following people:

my parents, Mr. and Mrs. Ronald and Annie Holmes
(I love and miss you);
my mother-in-love, Mrs. Mary Amerson McDougald;
my "pops," Mr. Arlee King
(who helped raise me right);
Rev. (Uncle) Robert Brantley;
and finally, to Bishop George D. Lee III.
These are people who made deposits into my life.

I also dedicate this book to my beautiful children,
Shekinah Joye and Daniel II,
and to my nieces and nephews,
Gloria, Demetrius, Tosha, Terrance, Jeffrey, Tamara,
Kymberli, Chanel, Danielle, Michelle, Charissa,
Cortney, LeVon, Tanesha, Jonathan, and Chris.
I love you all!

Table of Contents

Part 3: Friend or Foe?

Acknowledgments

This project has been a blessing to me. Even as I worked on it, God spiritually placed me back in my teen years so I could relate, accurately, to how you feel as a teen. I cried, I laughed, I repented, I rejoiced. I am amazed at the outcome and give all honor to God. His Word is true, and it will last forever.

I am thankful to my wife, Annette, and my children, Shekinah Joye and Daniel II. They allowed me to take time out and write this book to you. My wife exemplifies the love of Christ and taught me the true meaning of love.

My brothers and sisters: Patricia (Pat), Margo, Ronald Jr. (Jethro), Charlotte, James (Sherlock), Karon, and Antonio (Tony).

My mentors, Dr. Michael and Dr. Bernita Mitchell, who blessed me with their insight on the project and supported me in prayer. You two have been more than mentors; you have been friends and spiritual coverings at a very critical time in our lives and our ministry.

The people who shaped my Christian roots: Joe Boulware; Mr. John Atherton; Dr. Sam Davis (my other voice of wisdom); Teen Challenge in Chattanooga, Tennessee (they rebuilt my spiritual foundation); David Jones and Barbara McCullum (*true* friends); and Mike King (the greatest musician in the world!).

My "other parents" who helped raise me, Mrs. Robert Brantley, Mama Kay King and family, and Mr. and Mrs. Eli Bowden and family—thanks!

I want to also thank those powerful men and women of God who spoke into my and Annette's life over the years. Thank you, Dr. Tony Evans! The example of you and Dr. Lois has been priceless! Thanks you Dr. Frederick K.C. Price and Dr. Betty for your deposits and guidance. Thank you, Dr. I.V. Hilliard for your example and speaking into my mentor's life. Thanks to my pastor and father, Bishop Daniel Robertson, Jr. and Co-Pastor Elena. Wow! God directed me here just in time and revealed a true man and woman of God. You two and Assistant Pastor Kenneth Mitchell and Minister Audrea have been a contagious example of confidence in the Word of God and its power. That's why we are a debt-free ministry. Thanks for allowing Annette and I to flow in God's gifts.

Finally, I thank *you,* my ministry partners, for pulling on the gift inside me and challenging me to give you a word.

Foreword

Don't Buy the Lie is a book that I take great delight in forewording and giving my full stamp of approval.

Since I am the father of four, two teens and two preteens, I have dealt firsthand with much of what is addressed.

Pastor Holmes is a man of God, a loving husband and father. Also, he is a bona fide youth pastor and speaks experientially on subjects facing today's teens and preteens.

I have known Pastor Holmes for more than thirty years. I have seen firsthand the impact he's had on teens and youth. He and his lovely wife, Annette, have such magnetic and endearing personalities that make them so appealing to people everywhere.

This book is designed to expose the ploys of the enemy toward our youth while equipping them with the Word of God. It encourages them to find themselves through God's Word.

I would venture to say that this book is a must read for parents, potential parents, youth ministers, and anyone who loves God's children. It is a mighty weapon of warfare against the forces of evil that are set out to destroy our children.

Dr. Michael Mitchell

Pastor, Restoration Ministries International

INTRODUCTION

I Remember...

As I sit here in my study this overcast Saturday afternoon, I recall my teen years. Though they seem to be so long ago, some of the anxieties, embarrassments, and pains are still fresh in my mind. Hindsight is always 20/20, and it's natural to look back and say, "I wish I would have done this" or "If I had only said that, things would have been different." This book is for you who are going through those years right now. I merely want to share some of my wisdom (from experience) with you in hopes that you will not look back thirty years from now and say, "If only I had...."

Please take this book, read it, reflect on it, and read it again and again and again. Next, share it with someone you care about. I know if you read this with an open heart, God will speak to you and your life will be changed.

I am sharing some of my experiences with you so you can see the ramifications of making good and bad decisions and how they will shape your future. I am also sharing some of the stories I have heard from some of the hundreds of young people I've spoken to over the years at youth retreats, conferences, and workshops.

We live in a society with double standards, but as a child of God, there is only one standard, and that is the Word of God. God's Word says we are *in* the world but not *of* the world. My prayers are that you look around you with spiritual eyes, see what the world is offering you, and *Don't Buy the Lie!*

PART ONE

Who Me?

This section deals with you and just how wonderful you are. Society wants to make you believe you are nothing without "this" or "that," but the truth of the matter is that you are *awesome!* The things you face now are different than the things your parents or the generations before you faced simply because now it's *you* who are facing them. Rest assured, great wisdom comes from beheading the giants this world places before you and going through those valleys of loneliness and indecision, so listen to those people around you who are called and chosen to speak into your life. You *are* different, and when faced with the same trials that others face, because you are *you*, you will react differently. Refer to this section often to give you the spiritual booster you will need in the times the world wants to tell you to be "like Mikey."

ONE

Nothing New Under the Sun... (...yeah right!)

The thing that has been—it is what will be again, and that which has been done is that which will be done again; and there is nothing new under the sun (Ecclesiastes 1:9 AMPC).

I remember as if it were yesterday. Eddie, Jeffrey, Billy, and I were all in the locker room of Walker Jr. High in Fort Knox, Kentucky. We had just finished PE and were changing. The subject came up about girls, and we all started cracking on each other and laughing. We discussed who we had kissed and "felt up," and it was funny. We talked about the girls who were easy and those who were "teasers." It was like a "who's who" in the school we were attending. The music we jammed to back in the day was "Jungle boogie," "She's not just another woman," "Fire," and "Stay in my corner."

Some things have changed, yet some are still the same. Today, boys still talk about girls in the locker room and the level of their conversation is the same. Girls talk about boys in the locker room also, and I have discovered that they, too, talk about the boys who are the "easy" ones. The music young people are listening to is different. We hear lyrics like "I want to lick you up and down...till you say stop," "Truffle butter," "Back that thang up," and "I am getting so hot, I'm gonna take my clothes off." Hearing some of the music today scares me, and as I look at the "tube," my heart is broken. Yes, young people, you are under a great deal of pressure just as we were, but the pressure is different. Before, there were subtleties in satan's—I'm not using caps for his name on purpose—approach, but today there is no subtlety.

There's no wonder the US has the highest rate of sexually transmitted infections in the entire industrialized world, and one in four teens contract a STI every year, according to the website, Do Something (www.dosomething.org/facts/11-facts-about-teens-and-stds). Girls are under pressure to look like the "booty-shaking" girls on major music video channels. Sitcoms also captivate the attention of young people today. Young people are pressured to believe they must look picture perfect in order to be accepted. Most of the commercials on TV are geared toward the young, and they are sex-centered.

In viewing most of today's movies and television shows, we see the world system telling us how to dress and act, and the world's idea of how to do so is a direct opposite of what the Word of God says. Per the world's system, if a boy is not disrespecting his "ho" in front of his "peeps," he doesn't have a backbone.

Unfortunately, the females buy into it and allow the boys to say anything to and around them. Honey, if a boy uses profanity *to* or *around* you, he has no real respect for you, and without respect, there is no "love."

The Word says there is nothing new under the sun, and the Word is true. Temptation is not new, but with new technology come new *ways* of being tempted. In other words, the means of the temptation is new and much more provocative. We need to remember that satan's job is to take what God created and pervert it.

Before he fell, satan's name was Lucifer and he was the most beautiful and powerful angel (Ezekiel 28:12-19). He was the chief angel in charge of praise and worship. He was beautiful, and there was beautiful music in his every move. When satan rebelled, he was expelled from heaven because he perverted the gift God gave him, and it's been perverted ever since.

The devil does not make anything new; he takes what God has given us and perverts it. To put it simply, God gives us good music that lifts His name, and He creates (through people) beautiful love music, mellow jazz music, great country, rock, reggae, house, classical, and rap music that edifies Him.

The devil takes what was made to be good and changes the words, which distorts the original intent. It sounds good to the body but has no nutritional value to the spirit.

What we have to keep in mind is that just because it feels good to you, it may not necessarily be good *for* you. We will get into music in chapter ten.

I have come across thousands of young people in ministry, counseling, prisons, schools, workshops, and retreats and found that their desire to be accepted by others is the common thread that binds them all. The media has taken that desire and dictated to young people how their peers and society can accept them, and unfortunately, their view of acceptance is not God's view. Everyone wants to love and be loved, but society's view of love, because satan influences it, is the perverted view that always leads to pain.

Let's look in the Bible at an example of a young person, thought to be in love, being influenced in a perverse way. In 2 Samuel 13:1-6, 9-15 (NIV), the Word says this:

> *In the course of time, Amnon son of David fell in love with Tamar, the beautiful sister of Absalom son of David. Amnon became so obsessed with his sister Tamar that he made himself ill. She was a virgin, and it seemed impossible for him to do anything to her. Now Amnon had an adviser named Jonadab son of Shimeah, David's brother. Jonadab was a very shrewd man. He asked Amnon, "Why do you, the king's son, look so haggard morning after morning? Won't you tell me?"*
>
> *Amnon said to him, "I'm in love with Tamar, my brother Absalom's sister."*
>
> *"Go to bed and pretend to be ill," Jonadab said. "When your father comes to see you, say to him, 'I would like my sister Tamar to come and give me something to eat. Let her prepare the food in my sight so I may watch her and then eat it from her hand.'"*
>
> *So Amnon lay down and pretended to be ill. When the king came to see him, Amnon said to him, "I would like my sister Tamar to come and make some special bread in my sight, so I may eat from her hand."*
>
> *Then she took the pan and served him the bread, but he refused to eat..."Send everyone out of here," Amnon said. So everyone left him. Then Amnon said to Tamar, "Bring the food here into my bedroom so I may eat from your hand." And Tamar took the bread she had prepared and brought it to her brother Amnon in his bedroom. But when she took it to him to eat, he grabbed her and said, "Come to bed with me, my sister."*

"No, my brother!" she said to him. "Don't force me! Such a thing should not be done in Israel! Don't do this wicked thing. What about me? Where could I get rid of my disgrace? And what about you? You would be like one of the wicked fools in Israel. Please speak to the king; he will not keep me from being married to you." But he refused to listen to her, and since he was stronger than she, he raped her.

Then Amnon hated her with intense hatred. In fact, he hated her more than he had loved her. Amnon said to her, "Get up and get out!"

"No!" she said to him. "Sending me away would be a greater wrong than what you have already done to me."

There are a variety of things we can find by reading these verses but, for the time being, I want to focus on the third verse. Instead of Amnon, the son of the king, relying on his father or mother for advice in this situation, he relies on an "outsider." Even though the outsider was a relative, it was not mom or pop. This outsider was his cousin Jonadab. Jonadab was Amnon's father's much older brother's son, and he was a crafty man. That word *crafty* is the same word used in Genesis 3:1 when the Bible is discussing the serpent. I submit to you that the same demonic force that beguiled the woman in the Garden of Eden beguiled Amnon.

They were both challenged, just like Jesus (Matthew 4:1-11) with the lust of the eyes and the flesh and the pride of life. These are the only things the ruler of this world system has to offer. When the "serpent" tempted Eve, he discussed how the fruit looked (the lust of the eyes), how good it was as a food (lust of the flesh), and how it would make her wise like God (the pride of life). After considering this, she ate it (Genesis 3:1-6).

Amnon listened to what he thought was the voice of "reason." Jonadab was much older and more experienced. Amnon thought Jonadab to be in tune with the things around him, and Jonadab could be relied on to steer Amnon in the right direction. Amnon saw Tamar as beautiful (lust of the eyes), and he fell sick for her (lust of the flesh). The first thing Jonadab said to Amnon was a reminder of his status. "Man, you are a king's kid"—the pride of life—"Why are you down?"

When Amnon told Jonadab, "Man, my half sistah is PHAT, and I have to have her," Jonadab laid down a foolproof plan. He told Amnon to lie! Young people, if someone tells you something that is contrary to the Word of God, be like Joseph and *run*! If you are a born-again Christian, you must *plan* to sin. Sin does not come unexpectedly to the believer. An ungodly thought will try to plant itself in your mind, and if you entertain that thought, sin will follow. If you are not a Christian, you are still without excuse.

You have a conscience (Freud called it a super-ego) that speaks to you and tells you right from wrong. When you are battling within yourself whether to do something or not, that's the real you inside fighting with your flesh. My suggestion when that happens...listen to the inside!!

When Amnon finally got what he thought he could not do without, he hated it and wanted to be as far from it as he could.

I was watching Christian television this morning, and the host was discussing the plight of teens today. She stated that teens don't want to talk to their parents about things because parents will be too judgmental and not understand the teen's individual situation. That is an understandable reaction. I remember when I was young, I did not believe my parents would understand either until I had to trust them.

When I was in college, there was a person I just did not get along with and I decided I would "handle" the problem. I took one of my father's guns from home, and I had planned on using it to shoot this adversary. My best friend, David, found out I had the gun, and he stole it from me. He then gave it to his dad who gave it to my dad. When my dad showed me the gun, I froze! I did not know how he was going to respond. My father was an ex-drill sergeant, a golden glove boxer, and a war veteran. He was one for order and did not tolerate too much of anything. My dad came in the room and laid the gun down and asked if we could talk about it. He sat there and said nothing until I was through.

That shocked me because I was expecting to regain consciousness in the hospital or something. I had the opportunity to lie to my pops, but he trusted me enough to ask so I wanted to try something different...the truth.

Everything is the same yet so very different now. We live in an "instant" and "microwave" society now, and the things it took time to do when I was young take very little time to do today. Because of this, young people expect gratification instantly. If you are hungry, you open the fridge and get something out and stick it in the microwave. In a matter of seconds or minutes, you have a hot meal. When I was young, we had to turn on the oven and wait for it to get warm.

The difference between then and now is that food from the oven is more palatable than food from the microwave. This tells me that for things to be good *for* you and *to* you, it takes time.

I too am spoiled by the way we are satisfied so quickly today, but every once in a while, I go into the kitchen and turn on the oven. There is nothing like the smell of food cooking in the oven. Bread and eggs just doesn't taste the same in the microwave.

I have four vehicles, and I like good dependable transportation, but there is nothing like going for a walk with my family. Our society wants things *now* but the Word of God says to be patient and let patience have her perfect work so that you may be perfect (mature) and entire, wanting nothing (James 1:2-4 KJV). When we face trials and various temptations, according to James, we have an opportunity to mature if we remain patient and look to God for the way out and what is best for us.

Boys today play the same games to get what they want as we played when I was young. The only difference, once again, is the way they play the games. Unfortunately, the odds are a lot steeper today. With the onset of HIV and AIDS, the games are deadlier. Today, according to the Center for Disease Control (CDC), 25 percent of all new HIV infections in the United States are among people under twenty-five. We will discuss STDs in chapter five.

Over the years, I have discovered the importance of the Word of God and how it really applies to every aspect of my life. If I had known this when I was your age, I would not be writing this book; but this is giving you an advantage. You have someone who has traveled down the road already and knows where the potholes are, what exits to take, and which ones *not* to take. Listen to someone who knows where the weather turns bad, where the curves are, and how not to turn onto a dead-end street. Please take advantage of the Word of God and the person who has been down the road. While I am there, let me tell you of a vision I had some years ago.

I saw two roads: one was narrow, and the other was wide. From my point of view, the wide road was beautiful. It was well lit and wide enough for lots of people to travel.

I could see a big city a little down the road, and the city was large. I saw tall, well-lit buildings, and it was the type of place I would love to be. The other road had what looked like little lamps on the side of the road, and it seemed desolate. It seemed like not too many people traveled the road, and I could not see anything in the distance on that road.

Suddenly, an angel lifted me high above the roads. I heard him say, "The Lord wants you to see the whole picture." As I was taken up higher, it was as if my view became clearer. From a higher perspective, as I looked at the two roads, I saw something entirely different. The wide and beautiful road was lit only to what I *thought* was a city. It was like I was looking at a prop for a cowboy movie because the lights were as if they were pasted on a big slab of cardboard and there was nothing behind it but a very narrow alley. There was total darkness except for what looked like a burning furnace further down the road.

The other road that was lined with lamps suddenly began to widen, and the lamps grew taller until they were light posts. Further down the road, the posts stopped because on the horizon there was a beautiful bright light. As I looked down at the streets, I saw the purest gold I have ever seen. The angel then told me, "If you can see everything, you don't need faith."

Travel the road God chose for you, and it will lead you to victory. The road may not be the popular road, but it is the right road for you.

You know where you are right now. Are you on the road God ordained for you? If you ask, He will order your steps. His word is a lamp for your feet and a light for your path (Psalm 119:105). Stop here for a moment and pray this prayer with me:

Lord, You are all knowing and all seeing. I know there are things in my life that aren't pleasing to You. I ask that You forgive me and cleanse my heart. Am I on the right road, Lord? If so, forgive me for taking my eyes off You and looking at what I thought I was missing. If I am on the wrong road completely, Lord, I want to make a U-turn right now and get on the road You designed just for me. I believe Jesus is the Son of God, and I accept and acknowledge Jesus as my Lord and Savior. You said in Romans 10:9-10 that if I confess Jesus with my mouth and believe in my heart that God raised Him from the dead, I am saved. I receive my salvation now, and I thank You that I am a new creature traveling on the right road. This I pray and thank You in the name of Your Son, Jesus. Amen.

TWO

The Truth About You

You made all the delicate, inner parts of my body and knit me together in my mother's womb. Thank you for making me so wonderfully complex! Your workmanship is marvelous—how well I know it. You watched me as I was being formed in utter seclusion, as I was woven together in the dark of the womb. You saw me before I was born. Every day of my life was recorded in your book. Every moment was laid out before a single day had passed. How precious are your thoughts about me, O God. They cannot be numbered! I can't even count them; they outnumber the grains of sand! And when I wake up, you are still with me! (Psalm 139:13-18 NLT).

This is the part of the book where I get to talk about my favorite subject...*you!* I like this part because it's like moving into a new city and trying to get around without directions. Suddenly, someone gives you a map; you are "enlightened" and discover you are not as lost as you thought you were. The Word of God is the map you need, and as you read this chapter, you will discover things about yourself you never considered. Let's look again at our foundational scripture above.

Every time I read those verses, I get excited because I know the Lord is talking about you and me! In the King James Version, He said in verse fourteen that you are "fearfully and wonderfully made." I researched the words *fearfully* and *wonderfully* in *Strong's Concordance,* and they mean reverently set apart, shown marvelous and distinguished. Here in the New Living Translation, it says He made you "wonderfully complex." God took His time and made you. He did it for a purpose with a specific plan just for you.

As you remember from the book of Genesis, God made man from the dust of the earth and breathed life in him. Before He did this, He counseled with the Son and the Holy Spirit. He said, "Let us make man in our own image." We know dirt is not the image of God, so what was He talking about?

The answer is in John 4:24 where it says, "God is Spirit" (NLT). So, if God is Spirit and we are made in His image, we must be Spirit also, and when He breathed in Adam, He breathed "Adam" in the dirt that He molded! That "dirt" was merely Adam's "earth suit."

Just like an astronaut needs a space suit when he goes into space, while we are on this planet, we need an earth suit. More about that will come in chapter ten.

The enemy had it out for you at the beginning. Since your mother conceived you, satan has tried to take you out. How? I am glad you asked. The chance of a person winning the super lottery three times in a row is better than the odds of you being here. Let's look at this from a scientific standpoint. How many sperm cells does it take to make a baby?

The answer to that question is one. During intercourse, a male ejaculates three- to five-hundred million sperm cells inside a female. The acid in a woman's vagina kills half of the cells on contact. The other half make their way toward the fallopian tubes, some dying on the way. About 25 percent of those cells die before reaching the tubes, so we are down to about one-hundred to one-hundred-seventy-five million. When we get to the tubes, there is one egg in one of the tubes, and the sperm cells split up in search of the egg. Half of the sperm go to the wrong tube, and the other half go to the right tube, but many of them get misdirected and try to fertilize the wrong thing and die off. You did not die off. When the sperm finally get to the egg, there are close to sixty million cells trying to penetrate the egg at the same time. Many of the sperm cells die of exhaustion. You didn't! Finally, one of the sperm cells penetrates the egg (you), and the entire makeup of the egg changes so that no other sperm can get in.

When the fertilized egg travels down the tube and attaches itself to the uterus, the battle continues. The fertilized egg is treated as an invader, and the body tries to get rid of it. Even while your mother's natural defenses are combating the invader, God is forming you because you are the one in three- to five-hundred million sperm cells that made it. He is forming you as your mother is suffering from morning sickness. Your marker cells are giving each cell in your body a name and location, according to the intricate design of the heavenly Father as your mother grows larger and larger. As your mother gets gas and back pains, God is connecting your spine and your nervous system. He is setting in place His evangelist, His prophet, His psalmist, His pastor, His administrator, His minister of helps, His dancer, and His wonderfully working mouthpiece that will proclaim His Word to the nations.

You are *not* a mistake! Okay, you were adopted, you were a product of rape, you were a product of in vitro fertilization, you do not know who your natural parents are, or you never knew your dad. The means of your arrival has no bearing on your outcome. You are here by the divine design of the King of kings and the Lord of lords. You are not a zero, a loser, or a nothing. God does not make mistakes!

You were born for such a time as this to impact the world. There has never been, there is not, nor will there ever be anyone on the face of this earth like you. No one can ever do what you do the way you do it.

I was watching CNN earlier this week, and the reporter said a white woman in Great Britain had "mistakenly" gave birth to twin black babies. Honey, you can call it whatever you want, but it was time for those babies to come forth from the heart of the father.

If God can use a donkey to speak to his prophet, He can use a white woman to bring forth His appointed "ravens" to feed the nations. Those kids are blessed. I saw another couple that received in vitro fertilization who had twins. The irony of this situation is one twin is white and the other black. The boys are now in their teens, and they are both loved the same. Mom said God wanted them born and born then. These children are not mistakes because God makes all things work for the good to those who love Him and are called according to His purpose (Romans 8:28).

Psalm 139:16 says, "You saw me before I was born...Every day of my life was recorded in your book." This further proves there are plans for your life and you are not just wandering aimlessly in the universe without a purpose. I know, at times you feel inadequate, unloved, unwanted, and unimportant, but everything about you is proof of how much God really loves you. The fact that you are reading this book is proof of His handiwork.

The brain that you are using to process the shapes you see on this page is the most marvelous and complex configuration in the universe. The average brain is about three pounds but contains more than one-hundred billion nerve cells. Within those cells are more than a hundred-thousand billion protein molecules that record everything that has ever happened in your life. With that in mind, I am glad you are reading this book because now you will never forget it. God cares so much about you that He gave you a treasure between your ears that is more priceless than all the precious gems and metals of the world combined.

Who told you that you were to awaken today? Where's it written that you are to awaken tomorrow? Do you understand that the moment your heart first began to beat, it was one beat closer to its very last beat? Understand that each second you are alive is a second closer to your eternity. By the time you finish this book, you will be closer to eternity than you were at the onset. Your heart just beat, you just breathed, and each beat or breath brings you closer to your end in this mortal body.

Please understand, there is nothing written in any book nor is there a law written that says you should exist. It is only written in the heart of God and by His grace and mercy that you are here. This is *your* time! God brought you forth from His heart for such a time as this to bring *your* individual flavor to the world. The Word says we are to be the "salt" of the earth. Now is the time for you to be flavor, just like salt.

Salt in My Life

I remember, when I was in high school, I had a friend named Johannesburg Boulware. "Joe" was an awesome athlete. He was strong and fast and one of the best hurdlers in the state.

He was, because of his athleticism, very popular, but the greatest thing about Joe was his love for Christ. Joe *loved* Jesus and was not ashamed to tell anyone. He never beat anyone over the head with his Bible; instead, Joe "lived" the Word. He was lively and had fun with people, but there were things that others did that Joe would not do. His love for Christ was more important than his being accepted by people.

Joe had standards, and he did not waiver from them. God blessed Joe academically and athletically. Now Joe is a pastor and proprietor simply because of his decision to "sprinkle" where he was. He was salt, and because of his flavor, my life is better. I remembered the life and example Joe led and wanted the peace in my life that God gave him.

There was also Mr. John Atherton. Mr. Atherton was a math teacher at the high school I attended. He always wore a smile and had a kind word. There were times when I was down or in trouble and Mr. Atherton would take me into his class and talk to me. The way he took his time and listened to me during stressful times help mold my life. He would give me that gentle smile, and I was immediately at peace. Mr. Atherton *loved* the Lord, and part of his ministry was to "sprinkle" on the students and staff there at North Hardin High School. He had a peaceful spirit, and he imparted that peace with every handshake, pat on the shoulder, and gentle word he gave.

Look around for the "sprinklers" in your life. God strategically places them everywhere so we can be seasoned and, in turn, become the "seasoners." God knew before time began that you would need to be encouraged. He knew there would be pressures in your life that would make you question your existence and your reason for being, so He wrote Psalm 139 especially for you.

In verses 7 to 12 of the same Psalm, David acknowledged that he could not go anywhere to get away from the presence of God. There are times when we feel no one understands us and no one is there for us, but His Word says He will never leave us or forsake us (Joshua 1:5).

God said in Jeremiah that before he formed you in your mother's womb, He *knew* (was intimate with) you, and before you came forth, He sanctified you and ordained you a prophet to the nations (Jeremiah 1:5). We are all created to speak or proclaim the Word of the Lord in one fashion or another. Not everyone has to be behind the pulpit to proclaim the Word. We do it every day by living the life we live.

Now that you know you have a purpose and God loves you dearly no matter who you are and what you have done, it's time to apply your knowledge. Go back and read Psalm 139. Afterwards, read Jeremiah 1:4-10. God is not prejudiced. He is not moved by something as superficial as the color of skin or social status. The same faith others used to accomplish the miraculous then and now is available for you. The difference between you and any other mighty person of God is your level of faith.

To get "buff," one must go to the gym and work out. No one goes into the gym for the very first time and bench presses 1,000 pounds. It takes exercise to get to the 1,000-pound level. The same exercise necessary in the physical is necessary in the spiritual. You must exercise your faith to get to the 1,000-pound level. Get God's Word concerning you deep in your heart by reading it and meditating on the Word. It becomes real to you, and that's what builds your faith. By "exercising" your faith, you grow spiritual muscles that help you fulfill your purpose in life.

Now it's time to go to the throne and thank God for His enlightenment. Believe me, as I write this book, God is removing the scales from my eyes so I am discovering new levels of His wonderful power and love.

Stop here and pray with me:

Lord, I want to take time out to thank You for being so meticulous when You made me. Thanks for Your Word that reminds me how wonderful I really am. I will no longer disrespect You by thinking bad about Your creation and Your greatest miracle...me! I acknowledge my value and look to You for the fulfillment of my purpose here on earth, and I thank You for my uniqueness. In Jesus' name, amen.

THREE

How Proverbs 22:6 Applies to Me

> *Train up a child in the way he should go [and in keeping with his individual gift or bent], and when he is old he will not depart from it* (Proverbs 22:6 AMPC).

I chose to use the Amplified version of this verse because it sheds more light on the subject of training a child. Inside the brackets lies the secret of training up a child. It says that you train a child according to what is inside him or her. God is the one who reveals the gift. Allow me to tell you a bit about myself as an example.

I am the seventh of eight living children. I was considered the "runt" of the family because I weighed about as much as a bag of sugar. I was so small my nickname was "Dinky." My sister Charlotte revealed how I got my name. When I was born, my mother didn't know what she was going to name me. A nurse came into her room and said, "His name will be Daniel Solomon" and walked out. This nurse was never seen again.

My younger brother Antonio (Tony) and I used to go to church three times every Sunday. We would hit the hill from Rose Terrace in Fort Knox to Prichard Chapel at the beginning of another neighborhood, and we would spend all day at the church. We would attend the Catholic and Protestant services. We would, later, get on the bus that came through our neighborhood and go to Valley Station to Beth Haven Baptist Church. We liked the treats, but we were hungry for the Word and those days laid the foundation for our ministry. My mother and father never talked about eternal life, religion, or church. The fact is, we all went to Catholic church until my dad retired from the military in the mid '70s because most military families in those days were Catholic. We then attended a Baptist Church in Elizabethtown.

As I reflect upon those years, I remember the girls I used to communicate with through high school and college. I seemed to be attracted to older women because the girls my age were nice to "talk" to. It was like all of the nice and pretty girls wanted to cry on my shoulder. I used to spend countless hours walking around the neighborhood and on campus talking to some of the most beautiful females. My friends thought I was getting somewhere with them, but the fact was...I was just talking. They would open up to me and knew no one else would know. I would listen, and they liked that. In listening to them, I learned not just about them but about human nature.

I recall my parents would talk to me about their problems and I would think, *Why in the world are you discussing this with me?* But I discovered they were talking to the "Solomon" in me. Solomon was a discerner and was full of wisdom.

He was a problem solver, but he was wise enough to know that sometimes the best way to get to a good answer to someone's problem was to help them discover the answer on their own and just listen to the process. After years of reading the Word and listening to ministers preach and teach the Word of God, I did not depart from the way I was "trained." No, my parents did not teach me the Word of God, but they gave me the liberty to go out and learn.

My parents were also given to hospitality. As I was growing up, our home was never empty! Though I had seven other brothers and sisters, we always had room for others. We were not rich, but we always shared and never wanted for anything. My parents opened their hearts and doors to people all their lives.

When we were overseas, our home was open to soldiers who had no family there, and when we were stateside, we shared our home with the lonely and hurt. I learned hospitality from my parents, and that which I learned has helped my ministry tremendously. My wonderful wife and I have been married over thirty years, and in those years we have raised hundreds of children that call us Mom and Papa. We have housed families, couples, and individuals. We have sponsored students to come to the US and get an education, and it's all because of the way we were trained.

When I was younger, I was a gifted track athlete. I could jump like no other, and my talents got me far. My brothers and sisters were great athletes also because my father was a great athlete. I noticed something. My father was a golden-glove boxer and an extremely great swimmer, but not one of his kids boxed. We all know how to swim (some better than others), but the only sport all of the boys had in common was basketball. We would go to the gym and run people off the court—except for the Bowdens, of course...they were awesome, but we sometimes gave them a run for their money! The girls were track stars and majorettes. The fortunate thing about us was we were not "forced" to be athletes or to do what Dad had done. We did what we liked, according to our individual gifts, and our parents supported us. When my children were born, I did not immediately go out and get them track shoes (even though I wanted to). I will see their strengths and help them to develop in those areas.

Another aspect of "training up a child" is in the spiritual realm. When a person first becomes a Christian, the Word says, they are a new creature (2 Corinthians 5:17). We become "babies" born in a ministry. We need spiritual parents that can discern our gifts and place us where we will be most effective according to our gifts.

It is important to be placed in a growing ministry with people that will help you develop your gifts so you will not bring reproach upon your (spiritual) parents.

Another reason to develop your spiritual gift is no other human being that has ever existed is like you. There are things you can do that no one else in the history of the world can do because God does not mass-produce people. We learned in the last chapter that you are "fearfully and wonderfully made." God took His divine time making you with intricacies no one else possesses. Therefore, it is virtually impossible for me to reach the people you are designed to reach the way you reach them.

Some of the things your parents (natural or spiritual) make you do or perhaps will not allow you to do may seem crazy, but keep in mind it is all for a divine purpose. We don't always see or agree with how we are being brought up, but God gave us those parents to help us grow.

The discipline I received as a child helped me grow. I didn't think so when I received it, but as I look back, I see it helped mold me. Both my natural and spiritual parents were hard on me. They weren't perfect people, but the things I learned by watching and listening are priceless.

My previous spiritual father made me clean windows and toilets and change poopy diapers in order to be a minister of the gospel. My natural father made me scrub floors with toothbrushes, polish knobs and handles, and make my bed so good you could bounce a quarter on it, in order to go outside and play with my friends.

Did I learn discipline? Yes I did! Did I rebel? Yes I did! Did I always go back and do things the way I was told? Yes I did! I learned that parents aren't always right, but even in their "wrongness," I learned the right things. I remember when I was young, I tried to take short cuts for everything and always had to go back and do the task again the right way. My philosophy in life today was molded by the experiences of my childhood. I learned four important keys to success:

- Look at the way everyone else is dressing, acting, talking, and responding, and do just the opposite, and you will be in line with the Word of God.
- Be lazy! Do it right the first time, so you will not have to do it again.
- Whatever you are doing, do it so good that you will be proud to put your name on it and display it in the rotunda of the Capitol Building in Washington, DC.
- If you can't do it in the presence of the Lord...don't do it!

It was not by chance that people like Bill Gates, Tiger Woods, Oprah Winfrey, and Mary Lou Retton excelled in their respective fields. They knew they had a gift planted on the inside, and that gift was nurtured and watered. Now they are reaping the benefits of tapping in on the reason they are here.

Some people, even though they have not publicly recognized the Lord as the planter of their gift, knew it at an early age and exercised that gift while others awakened and later realized their gift. Whatever the case, we are all blessed with a gift and a reason for being.

What is it that you find easy to do? What is it that you enjoy doing while others might consider it boring, tedious, or dangerous? Just as the scripture states, we all have an individual gift and by tapping into it and dedicating that gift to the Lord and developing it to glorify Him, we will not only find success but fulfillment in life (Proverbs 22:6 AMP).

There are millions of talented people throughout the world who are what the world would call successful. A vast majority of those people are not fulfilled, and the reason is simple. All the money in the world cannot bring you inner peace, and there is no satisfaction in perverting the gift given to you by God for selfish gain.

Look at most of the people in the news or on the cover of magazines today. One multimillionaire is so concerned about superficial things that he has received numerous plastic surgeries to make him look different in hopes of finding peace. Other talented and famous multimillionaires marry three and four times, trying to find happiness.

The ironic thing about the whole situation is some are still married to spouse number two and openly committing adultery with future spouse number three and expecting God's blessings on their mess. The press calls the romances "storybook." Other prominent sports figures cannot stop beating on their wives. The troubling thing about these situations is young people look to these "Jonadabs" for guidance and idolize them.

Please hear me—you will never be satisfied with anything apart from the will of God, and no one can bring you satisfaction or fulfillment but God. We try so hard to find our completeness in things and people without considering the one who made us. We will learn more about ourselves as we read the instructor's manual, which is the Bible, and have a personal relationship with God, the manufacturer.

Training up a child is not enough. That child must be trained according to their individual gift *and* in the fear and admonition of the Lord.

Just look at all of the unhappiness in Hollywood and on basketball courts, football fields, and concert stages because people have prostituted the anointing in their lives. Who is the giver of the gift? If the gift came from God, who would better know the best use of the gift than the Giver? God created us, and then He gave us each an individual gift.

When we acknowledge God with our gift and learn how to use it effectively, our gifts will be recognized by all and it will bring joy to ourselves and others. Not only will our gift bring us joy, but it will also bring joy to the world around us and bring glory to God.

Now is the time to tap into your gift. If you aren't sure of the gift placed within you, do an inventory. Look at the things you enjoy doing and you find easy. Think of the times when you are most creative. Ask people very close to you what they see as an asset you possess.

God said in His Word that He delights in the prosperity of His people (Psalm 35:27) and that His people make their way prosperous by meditating on and doing His Word (Joshua 1:8). He also gave us, as the "trainees," an obligation. We must be trainable!

We must allow ourselves to submit to the authority of the trainer. God's Word says that rebellion is as the sin of witchcraft (1 Samuel 15:23). Like I stated before, sometimes your "trainer" may make demands of you that you do not like or you do not see the logic behind. *Do it anyway!* Why? If it is not contrary to the Word of God and poses no threat to you or others, if you do it, it will build character. Don't gripe or complain while doing it, just do it and thank God for the victory and for molding you into His likeness during the experience.

Now is the time to go again before the throne of the Lord. He is not only the author and finisher of our faith, but He is the creator of our destiny and a rewarder of those who diligently seek Him. Let's pray:

Lord, I thank You for taking Your time and making me with great precision. I also thank You for the gift You placed within me. I want to use the gift You gave me to glorify You. I choose to listen and submit myself to those You have chosen to speak into my life as my "trainers," and I thank You for them. In Jesus' name, I pray, Amen.

FOUR

The Esau Syndrome

Watch out for the Esau syndrome: trading away God's lifelong gift in order to satisfy a short-term appetite. You well know how Esau later regretted that impulsive act and wanted God's blessing—but by then it was too late, tears or no tears (Hebrews 12:16-17 MSG).

In chapter one, we discussed the problems with instant gratification and how it may fill the desire for now but leave a sour taste in your mouth later. We discussed Amnon and how he finally got what his flesh desired but hated it after he got it. Esau was Jacob's twin but the elder brother, and he was a skilled hunter. Jacob was quiet and peaceful (Genesis 25:27). Since Esau was the eldest, he had the right to receive God's blessings from his father, Isaac. The scripture says that they had battled one another while they were in the womb—Jacob came out of his mother's womb holding on to the heel of Esau.

One day, Esau had come in from the field and he was extremely hungry. I am sure anyone can relate to that. There are times in our lives when our flesh is *screaming* out for satisfaction, and we will do anything to satisfy it. Esau was hungry. He was so hungry that he was willing to do anything to get some food. My question to you is, are you willing to give your future up for temporary satisfaction?

Esau did. He gave up his future blessings for immediate gratification.

We previously talked about how the society we live in today is considered a "microwave" society. We get our food much faster in the microwave than cooking it in the oven or over the stove.

There's something special about taking your time and cooking food. Anything a person puts forth effort to do, when it is accomplished, it's more rewarding. I can recall countless times when I should have waited on something, but instead, my impatience got me something I regretted. We oftentimes "see" something we must have, and without planning, get it "our way."

Esau was sure to get food eventually, but he wanted it then and there, and without thinking things through, he sold his future for momentary gratification. How can this apply to you? Let's look at a scenario.

Jessica is a senior in high school. She is right on the border of passing or failing this class, and she has a paper due. If she does well on the paper, she will pass the class and be able to graduate. If she fails the paper, she will fail the class. She was raised to "do what you have to do so you can do what you want to do" (Denzel Washington), so she knows how to prioritize. Robert, her boyfriend (remember Jonadab?), wants her to go to a party. It is slated to be the best party of the year, and everyone will be there. He pressures her into going to this party for a few hours, explaining that she "needs" a break and they will not stay long.

They go to the party, and it's a blast! They have the time of their lives until, on the way home, Jessica realizes that Robert is too drunk to drive. She ends up not having enough time to finish the paper, thus failing the class and not being able to graduate.

It doesn't even have to be that drastic. Another scenario could be a person that wants some basketball shoes so bad that they steal them or "jack" someone for a pair. Getting a high-interest loan or a payday loan is another way of selling your "birthright" for instant gratification. Prisons are filled with people who traded their birthrights for instant gratification. Once again, we are a spirit, we have a soul (intellect, emotions), and we live in a body (earth suit), so who is in control?

In the case of Esau, the "Jonadab" was actually Jacob's mother. She was the person who told Jacob how to get over on his father and steal Esau's birthright. We have to be careful of those speaking into our lives.

There is another example of wanting to satisfy a short-term appetite in Acts chapter four. The entire church was giving so that everyone would have enough. The Word says in verse 34 that there was no one needy because all the people shared. The people would sell their property and take the money to the apostles so it could be distributed. In chapter five, we find two people who wanted instant gratification. A couple, Ananias and Sapphira, decided they would hold back some of the money and lie to the apostles. Because of their lies, they literally dropped dead. Sin has its own consequences.

God doesn't have to punish a person for sinning. Just like doing the right thing has its own rewards, sin has its own consequences and costs. Eventually, the price has to be paid.

Another example is Judas Iscariot. He was the treasurer for the Son of God, but he was also stealing from the treasury. He literally sold his soul and his eternity for thirty pieces of silver and the money he was stealing from the treasury. The pain and guilt of his sin caused him to hang himself.

Finally, there was the man who the Lord called "the prodigal son." This man went to his father and asked for his inheritance. After receiving it, the young man went and wasted all he had until he was broke and eating with pigs. This young man traded his inheritance for instant gratification. It is great that the story didn't end there. When he realized how foolish he was, the young man decided to go back home. The wonderful thing about it is, when he came close to his house, the father saw him and ran to him, blessing him.

It is good to know we have a God who doesn't beat us to death with our wrongs but, instead, loves us to life! There is a time and season for everything, and we must learn patience. Jacob benefitted from Esau's impatience and desire for instant gratification.

In My Life...

There was a time in my life when I was a thief and a drug dealer. I was trading my inheritance for instant gratification only to find I was never really satisfied. There was also a time when I was addicted to crack. We lost everything we had because of my desire for a high I would never experience again. All of that was because I was trading my inheritance for the "moment."

Right now, there is a broken heart reading this book. You are thinking of the things that you have done and the many times you have failed God, others, yourself. You think there is no way anyone could ever love you, and you don't blame them.

I was there as well, and I realized, through my wife, that God will never leave or forsake me! There is someone knocking on the door to your heart right now. Someone in your family who is telling you about God. Someone at your church or job or maybe someone at your school who constantly tries to tell you about God and what God has for you.

The best people to talk to in times of strong desire (impulse) are, quite often, not your friends. In times when your flesh (earth suit) is in control and wants instant gratification, those your age and in your sphere of influence are going through the very same things, so you must confide in this order:

- God! If you have a relationship with Jesus Christ, all you really have to do is talk to "Dad." The *awesome* thing about God is that wherever you are, He is there! All you must do is acknowledge His presence in your every situation, and He will come in and give you peace in the situation.
- Parents, if those lines of communication are open. They brought you forth. Trust in God who is in them, and live through everything you know they are going to say that you know isn't from God.
- Mentor—someone you trust to speak into your life, someone you respect enough to be real with.
- Counselor. There is nothing wrong with talking to a counselor. As a counselor and a minister, I have

someone to whom I release and refresh. Everyone needs someone in whom to confide.

I overcame by the grace of God and by being real with myself, my wife, and my God. There are quite a few people who didn't make it through the things I "conquered" on the way to becoming "Pastor Holmes," and He is still working on me. I thank God for Jesus and the blood that cleanses us from all unrighteousness.

Now is the time to go again before the throne of the Lord. Even though Esau and Jacob separated for a season, they reconciled. God is a God of restoration. Let's pray:

Lord, I thank You for teaching me, through Your Word, to wait. I see there is no reason to sell myself short for instant gratification because I know that You will give me what I need and desire in Your time. Thanks for knowing me completely and intimately enough to know my thoughts and desires even before I ask, and I thank You for the opportunity to exercise patience. I pray this in Jesus' name, Amen.

PART TWO

What About Sex?

(Four reasons to chill and one to freeze!)

This section deals with four reasons why you should not stress yourself about or allow yourself to be pressured into premarital sex. The ramifications of premarital sex are discussed in this section with a Biblical basis for each. Also included are some personal testimonies of those who waited and those who didn't. Please take your time and prayerfully digest this section so you will not fall victim to the tricks of the enemy and sell yourself short because God has given you a gift that the world wants to take away before it is time to release it.

FIVE

Where Your Body Goes...

Daughters of Jerusalem, I charge you by the gazelles and by the does of the field: do not arouse or awaken love until she desires (Song of Solomon 2:7 NIV).

Have you ever seen a pound cake made from scratch? You mix several different ingredients together that would normally taste a bit bland or even gross if eaten individually, and together they create the most scrumptious thing you could imagine. I think the best time to eat a piece of pound cake is hot from the oven. Let's say, for the sake of illustration, you were hungry for a hot piece of lemon pound cake (my favorite), and you asked your mom to make you one. You watch her put the ingredients together and mix them in the bowl. She greases the pan, pours in the batter, and then places it in the oven. She tells you she has to go to the store to get some ice cream to go with the cake, and the cake should not be disturbed until the timer goes off or it will be ruined.

You know this cake is going to be the bomb because it was made just for you. As the minutes go by, your anticipation stirs. You want that cake, and you can smell the aroma as it fills the entire house. You turn the oven light on and see how beautiful it has risen, but the timer has not gone off yet so you wait. As the aroma intoxicates you, your mouth begins to salivate and you begin to reason with yourself. "Did she start the timer as soon as she put the cake in, or did she wait a few minutes? I don't really need ice cream. Yeah, as I recall, she put the bowl and stuff in the dishwasher and even washed her hands before she started the timer, so the cake is actually closer to ready than the timer says. What is ten minutes going to hurt? It *looks* ready and *smells* ready, so it has to *be* ready."

Quickly, you take the cake from the oven and do just like you saw your mom do in the past. You run the butter knife around the sides and slightly hit the sides to loosen it from the pan. You get a large plate and put it on top of the cake pan and turn the cake over. You feel the cake as it transfers to the plate, and you sigh. As you lift the cake pan from the plate, your heart sinks. Half of the cake is still in the pan, and the dough is raw in the middle of the cake. The cake is ruined! You try to put it back in the pan to allow it to finish cooking, but it just gets worse. The cake falls, and it burns on the outside before it is finally cooked on the inside. It's just not the same.

The beauty is gone, the goodness is gone, and it smells rather burnt, all because you took the cake out before it was time.

That is how it is with sex. God created sex as something beautiful and shared in a monogamous marriage relationship. He placed all of the ingredients of sexual pleasure inside you along with the tools for reproduction. He put you in the "oven" of this world to bring forth a gift when the timer goes off. This world system is governed by our senses, and satan uses "Jonadabs" like the media to arouse the sensuality within us. The problem arises when we follow sensuality without using common sense.

Scientifically, our bodies go through a stage called puberty, and afterwards, we are ready to have a baby. During those changes that occur in our bodies, our minds search out to find meaning and acceptance for the way we feel. One moment we are okay, then the next moment we aren't. The zits, the hair growing in unusual places, the lack of hair growing while it is on others, the beginning of a menstrual cycle, the changes in voice tones and feeling uncoordinated at inappropriate times. All the while we see "buff" men on the tube and beautiful half-naked women and think we are supposed to be like that.

The enemy, through the media, uses a tool called "bandwagoning," which states, "Everyone else is doing it, so you should too." Because of this, your peers will lie about sex to pressure you into doing something you or they aren't ready for.

During the puberty stage, we are not really "cooked" yet. We look like we are ready to be adults, and others may sense the differences in us and like those differences, but on the inside, the dough is still raw. We are not emotionally ready for a physical relationship.

Remember back in chapter one when I said satan perverts all that is good? He does this with sex also. In beer commercials, car commercials, and even soft drink commercials, satan uses sex to sell the products. The lie he is trying to plant in your head is "this is sexy, and if you want to be sexy, get this."

According to Genesis 3:16, because of the sin of Adam, a woman's desire and longing is to have and be with a man. The painful thing about the whole situation is that a female will make sacrifices to get what she ultimately desires, which is love.

What most people in this world think is love is actually not love. Love is not about how we feel because feelings can change like the weather. Love is not dictated by our senses. The Word of God says that God so *loved* the world (prized, was committed to, obligated to) that He *gave* His only Son (John 3:16 AMPC).

Most adults cannot tell the difference between love and lust, so for teens, it is much more difficult. I will tell you the difference in a nutshell. Love is giving while lust is taking.

Another thing the world system will not tell you about sex is the spirituality of the act itself. The world harps on the sensual side of sex without telling the whole story.

When you physically give yourself to someone, you are actually *giving* yourself to him or her and you become one flesh.

Not only are you joined physically, but spiritual deposits are also made into each partner, one from the other. This is the way sex was designed by God and the reason monogamous sex with your spouse is so important.

What do you want to do in life? What accomplishments do you want to make? Why are you in school? What are your goals and aspirations in academics or athletics? I promise you this—if you become physically involved with someone while you are trying to pursue a goal, you will never reach the level of your potential because the person will take your eyes off the prize.

How can I say that? Easy! I've witnessed it personally and have seen it happen to others as an educator, a counselor, and a youth pastor.

I remember this young lady I counseled was one of the best athletes I had ever seen, and she was also academically fit. The problem was, she had this boyfriend when she was in high school. They became sexually involved, and she was in "love." The first thing that went down was her grades. He was a dropout and wanted to spend time with her, so she skipped school a lot. She was kicked off the team. This young woman could have gone to any college she desired on a basketball scholarship, but she took her eyes off the goal. She told me that she could not keep her mind off him, and when they were apart, she thought of him constantly. She caught him in bed with one of her best friends, and the relationship ended, but she became suicidal.

This is what I have come to understand, both in my personal life and in talking with other spiritual counselors. When you give yourself physically to a person, you give them a part of your soul also, and that part of your soul, which other person has, longs to be with the rest. This is the reason why a person can be thinking about their lover, and the next thing they know, the phone rings or there is a knock on the door and it is them. I can be hard at work and begin to think of my sweet and lovely wife, and the next thing I know, the phone rings and it's her. The reason this happens is because my body has been there. We have become one, and that part of me that is with her wants to be with the rest of me. Though we are apart, we are still together because the two of us became one flesh.

When you give yourself to another before it's time, you awaken things within you that you are not mature enough to deal with; in other words, the cake is done on the outside but it is still raw on the inside. Don't allow premarital sex to take your eyes off what God has called you to do because where the body goes the soul will follow.

Now is the time to go before God and ask Him to help us wait for the "timer" in our lives and not yield to the pressures of this world. Let's pray:

> *Father, I thank You that I am made with a purpose and You created me for love. Help me to tell the difference between love and lust. I desire to achieve Your purpose for my life, and I covenant with You now that I will not allow sex or the sensuality of this world to distract me. I thank You for the gift of the Holy Spirit within me who will help me stay strong. This I pray in Jesus' name, Amen.*

SIX

STIs? You're Buggin' Man... Not Me!

For the lips of a loose woman drip honey as a honeycomb, and her mouth is smoother than oil; but in the end she is bitter as wormwood, sharp as a two-edged and devouring sword. Her feet go down to death; her steps take hold of Sheol (Hades, the place of the dead). She loses sight of and walks not in the path of life; her ways wind about aimlessly, and you cannot know them. Now therefore, my sons, listen to me, and depart not from the words of my mouth. Let your way in life be far from her, and come not near the door of her house [avoid the very scenes of temptation], lest you give your honor to others and your years to those without mercy...and you groan and mourn when your end comes, when your flesh and body are consumed (Proverbs 5:3-9, 11 AMPC).

I remember talking to a young man who had just been treated for a sexually transmitted disease. He was totally confused how it had happened. He said, "I can't believe this happened to me. That girl was fine. She was nice and quiet." Also, a young lady once told me she thought she could trust the man that gave her genital herpes. I have sat across the desk from people who just didn't get it. Sexually transmitted infections have no face and are no respecter of persons. Once you leave the protective arms of God, you are playing Russian roulette with your life.

What are my intentions in this chapter? I intend to scare the *hell* out of you! It's not fun waking up in the morning and going to use the bathroom and the pain you feel as you urinate is so awful you want to scream. How about looking in your underwear and finding yellowish-green pus? Perhaps you would enjoy discovering sores all around your genital area or on your lips and in your mouth.

You go to the doctor, and he or she tells you that you have something that cannot be treated and that those sores will come and go occasionally. All the doctor can do is give you something for the discomfort. When the sores surface, don't have sex with anyone because they can get them. All of this because you misused the gift that God gave you for your spouse in marriage.

God's word says in Proverbs 5:11, "And you groan and mourn when your end comes, when your flesh and body are consumed" (AMPC). What does this mean? In the latter stages of AIDS, you get sores; with syphilis, you get sores; with herpes, you get sores. Where? On your flesh! The Word says your flesh and body are consumed.

Please understand the Word before you. She or he may look good, smell good, say the right thing, dress right, be smart—they can be everything you have ever wanted and they can kill you! This person is all that and a bag of chips yet more deadly than poison!

You never know who can burn you. Do not be deceived by someone's outer appearance. The word of God says, "The lips of an adulteress drip honey and her speech is smoother than oil; but in the end she is bitter as gall, sharp as a double-edged sword. Her feet go down to death; her steps lead to the grave" (Proverbs 5:3-5 NIV). We will look at the word *adultery* in the next chapter, and we will discover that you don't have to be married to commit adultery.

With most sexually transmitted diseases (STIs), men know within three to ten days that something is wrong, but women can go months without knowing.

When a girl gets a sexually transmitted disease from a boy, there is no way the boy doesn't know he is "burning." In essence, he does not care at that point as long as he gets "his." A girl may have a STI and not know it and, depending on how sexually active she is, she can give it to many others.

Society tells us to "wrap it up" and be safe, but that is far from the truth. Wearing a condom during sex is as effective as putting a bandage on a compound fracture! Condoms do not protect you from genital warts and herpes. Condoms do not protect you from crabs. Condoms do not protect you from hepatitis B or mononucleosis.

When you have sex with someone, you are not just having sex with that one person. You are actually having sex with that person and everyone that person has had sex with and *their* partners, and *their* partners, for the last ten years. The only "safe sex" is no sex until marriage and then marry someone who holds the same values of purity that you hold.

To clear this picture up for you, let's look at this scenario. Say, for instance, you were a virgin and you had sex with a boy. This boy was not a virgin. He had sex with one other girl, but she had twenty-five other partners. Out of those twenty-five partners, one was a bisexual and another was a junkie who used dirty needles. Even though you were pure and your partner was "close" to pure, you were infected with a disease that will kill you. Why? You will die because of the partners of the other person your sex partner had sex with. They carried the disease and gave it to your partner, who, in turn, gave it to you.

You defiled the temple of God and have left the protection of God's umbrella. Please understand that satan is waiting for the opportunity to destroy you. The tool satan uses is simple. He tells you that it will not happen to you.

Do you know that satan is tempting you the same way he tempted Jesus after Jesus was baptized? When Jesus went into the wilderness to be tempted, satan took Him up on a very high mountain and showed him all the kingdoms of the world and their splendor, magnificence, preeminence, and excellence. And he said to Him, "these things, all taken together, I will give you if you prostrate yourself before me" (Matthew4:8-9 AMPC).

Understand that satan is placing you on the top of that mountain continuously and offering you the riches of this world system, but the things he offers are only sensual. They can only please the senses and solely satisfy the lust of the eyes, the lust of the flesh, and the pride of life. The irony of it all is you will never be completely satisfied.

You will try and try again and never be satisfied with your pursuits. Sex is more addictive than drugs and the most effective tool satan has in his arsenal. Look at the television. Most of the commercials on it use a good-looking male or female to sell their goods. They try to suggest that if you want this kind of person in your life, you need this product.

The shows geared toward teens today promote sensuality, promiscuity, perversion, instant gratification, and addiction.

The television will ask you to "go to our website" where you will get another dose of perversion.

How many "reality" shows have you seen where they take you into a STI clinic and talk to people who have contracted a STI because they got drunk on some beer they saw advertised on television? How many shows have you seen where they interview AIDS patients who candidly discuss how they contracted the disease. Television will sell you sex but will *never* tell you the real price you have to pay.

As a Christian, when you commit a sexual sin, the Word says you are sinning against your own body. The Word also says that when you are tempted, He will give you a way of escape (1 Corinthians 10:13). Let's think about it while looking at another scenario.

You have this "friend" you really like, and she calls you one night. She is a very nice girl, but she does not go to church. She tells you her parents are gone for the evening, and she doesn't want to stay in that big house alone, so she was wondering if you wanted to come over and bring some movies. You just returned home from Bible study, and the lesson was about Joseph and Potiphar's wife. The Word is fresh on your heart, and the choice is yours to go or not. What satan will do is tell you that you are doing a good thing by going to keep this girl company. The truth of the matter is that when you were talking to her on the phone, you knew there was something "different" about the conversation. You decide to do her the favor of keeping her company.

You had the option to leave, but you chose to go on in when she answered the door with a mini skirt and tube top on.

You begin to watch the movie, and she moves close to you and begins to touch you in places that cause sensations you have never experienced.

She says to you that she knows you are a virgin and that's okay because she will take her time and rock your ever-loving world. You really like this girl and like how you are feeling at this point, so you give in.

Three days later, you feel a strong stinging while you are urinating. The pain is so unbearable that you could scream and you don't know what to do. Four days later, you begin to itch in your groin area and the itching gets worse and worse. You finally go to the doctor and discover you have gonorrhea and crabs, and they both were contracted sexually. Did God make a way of escape for you? Look back at the beginning of this scenario and count the escape routes God made for you. I counted five!

When you became one with Christ:

- Everything you do...He is there.
- Everywhere you go...you take Him.
- Everything you say...He hears.
- Everything you watch...He is subjected to as well.
- Everything you listen to...He hears as well.

God said in His Word that your body is the temple of the Holy Spirit who is in you (1 Corinthians 6:19). God wants to reach people through you. He wants to use your personality and the gifts He blessed you with to save the lives of millions. Can He use you if you are dead?

On the other hand, satan desires to take your life. The main objective of the enemy is to ruin you. He gets great pleasure if he blocks your blessings and destroys your testimony. Don't give him the opportunity to cut your life short because of a few moments of sin.

Finally, the Word says to avoid the very scenes of temptation. In both scenarios, temptation was not avoided and destruction followed. When you have premarital sex, you give your honor to others instead of your spouse. We will also discuss that in the next chapter.

In chapter four, you found out that premarital sex could make you take your eyes off of your goals because of the spiritual aspects of a physical union.

In this chapter, you found out that not only are there spiritual ties to sex but also, if you leave the umbrella of protection God supplies, you are subject to diseases that can ultimately kill you. Listen to the Spirit of God speaking to you through these pages and wait. Before we go any further, let's pray:

Lord, I thank You for the gifts You entrusted me with, and I desire to use them to glorify You. Your Word says that You live on the inside of me. I don't understand it all, but that's fine because I have faith in You. Because You live in me, everywhere I go, You are there too. I don't want to take You anywhere that would grieve You, and I don't want to do anything You wouldn't ordinarily do, so speak to my heart of hearts and direct me. You also gave me the gift of choice, Lord, and today I choose to obey Your Word and stay pure. In Jesus' name, I pray, Amen.

SEVEN

That Little Bambino

I will not show my love to her children because they are children of adultery. Their mother has been unfaithful and has conceived them in disgrace. She said, "I will go after my lovers who give me my food and my water, my wool, my linen, my oil and my drink." She will chase after her lovers but not catch them; she will look for them but not find them (Hosea 2:4,5,7).

I think I may need to define what the Bible calls "adultery" before I get into this chapter. Adultery is defined as whoredom in all its forms as well as unchastity (premarital relations, sexual impurity, and lustful desires under whatever name) (J.P. Lange, *A Commentary*). Not only is adultery forbidden, but also fornication and all kinds of mental and sensual uncleanness. All impure books, songs, pictures, etc., that tend to inflame and corrupt the mind are against this law (Adam Clark, *The Holy Bible with a Commentary*). This in-depth definition of the word *adultery* dispels any idea that you have to be married to commit adultery.

When Adam sinned in the Garden of Eden, the curse placed upon the woman was that she would *desire* and *crave* her husband. A female's natural instinct is to have the love of a man. Today, things are the same as the days of old. A woman will sell herself for love and *things*. Society and bandwagoning says you have to have this and that or you do not fit in. Today's teens want the fine things in life, and because of the microwave society we live in, they do not want to wait for them. A girl sees a good-looking, "edgy" guy or a popular one who is "iced-out," and she wants him. Her "Eve" nature kicks in, and her desire is for him.

One thing a girl must remember is that a boy ultimately wants sex, and he will do whatever he needs to do to get what he wants. The thing a girl wants is love. She will sacrifice everything she has and everything she *is* to get what she wants...even her body.

During the teen years, young people are "egocentric," which means they think all eyes are on them. They are mainly concerned with self, and love is "selfless," so teens are generally incapable of real love.

Lines like "If you really loved me" and "I will love you forever" are lines boys will use to tear down girl's defenses. What happens, the girl will use sex to get love and the boy will use love to get sex. Who loses?

The girl loses every time because she has given the boy something she cannot get back, and nine months later out comes the "little bambino." Whose responsibility is the child if the girl gets pregnant? He can go on his merry way as if nothing ever happened and pursue another conquest while she carries the baby or chooses to kill it through abortion.

When I was coming up, I knew I had a gift of writing, so I used it to my advantage. I was also a very patient person when it came to getting what I wanted. I always worked hard.

I remember going into the training areas at Fort Knox and shining the trainees' shoes for them and also taking my Polaroid camera and taking pictures of them for money so I could buy things. I would also go to the officers' apartments and wash cars for money. My parents instilled in me a work ethic that guides my life today. I liked pretty girls, so I would write poetry to them and buy them gifts. I would be sweet to them because I ultimately wanted to get under their skirts. I would listen to them, talk to them, and sing for them...*anything* it took to reach my goal. I liked a challenge, and with some girls, I waited for over a year to get what I wanted. When I got what I wanted, they lost my respect and my interest. I then looked for another conquest. It's no different today. Some boys are patient and some aren't, but the bottom line is they all want the same thing.

I stated previously that a girl ultimately wants love. Just like the boy, she will go to extremes to get what she wants. She will sacrifice her body for the sake of love but will ultimately be grossly disappointed to find out she was merely a conquest. She loses more because she gave this boy her most prized possession (her virginity) in order to receive something he is not able to give.

Another fallacy the enemy plants in the minds of young people is that bad things only happen to other people. *It can never happen to me* is the thought of most young people. I was looking at some statistics published by the CDC in 2001. Keep in mind, I said the girl is the loser in the "game."

Here are some startling numbers I discovered:

- Approximately 5 percent of every hundred teen girls in America have had a baby.
- 7 percent of the girls in the US have had sex before age thirteen.

- 14.2 percent of the teens in the US have had more than four sex partners.
- 45.6 percent of students have had sex.
- Nearly 5 percent of students have been pregnant or got someone pregnant at least once.
- In 1998, there were 775 abortions per 1000 live births in girls age fifteen or younger.
- The US has the highest adolescent pregnancy rate among developed countries in the world with over 800,000 teen pregnancies per year.

(Source: Youth Risk Behavior Surveillance System, Centers for Disease Control & Prevention, 2001 Survey.)

Don't let satan lie and tell you that it cannot happen to you because it can. Once you are out of the will of God, you are no longer under His "umbrella" of protection. If you get from under God's umbrella, satan can rain down on you. Psalm 91:1 (AMPC) says, "He that dwells in the secret place of the Most High shall remain stable and fixed under the shadow of the Almighty [Whose power no foe can withstand]." The definition of *secret,* according to *Strong's Concordance,* is something to cover, hide, to protect.

When we make a decision to go away from God's protection, we open ourselves up to the devastations satan has planned for us. Just like God has plans for us, satan also has plans. The plans satan has for us are to steal, kill, and destroy (John 10:10). What satan wants to do is steal your destiny and your joy, kill your hopes, and destroy your future.

Think of all the young ladies you know who have dropped out of school or were potential academic or athletic stars but whose hopes were crushed by an unexpected pregnancy.

I did an internship in a school in Georgia where one student had three different girls pregnant at the same time. Another young girl contacted me via email in December and asked me if it was true that God punishes us for sin. I explained to her that we simply reap the consequences of our decisions when we get from under the umbrella. This young lady was afraid God would make her unborn child "retarded" or deformed" because she had sex outside of marriage. People from her church had told her this, and she was perplexed.

I've witnessed hundreds of young girls' destinies crushed by an unexpected pregnancy by someone they thought really loved them. A vast majority of the time, the girl is left alone with the child while the boy goes on his merry way, not taking responsibility.

God already told you in Psalm 139:1-17 how He took His time making you and how precious you are.

Focus on what you really want out of life. Put love in the oven or the slow cooker and not in the microwave. If it's love, allow it to cook slowly so the flavor of love can fill the air and it cooks evenly throughout. If you microwave love, it may be hot on the outside but still undone and cold on the inside or turn out rubbery and tasteless.

Son, do not be snared by that mischievous girl who tells you how you "got it going on" because God warns you about that throughout the Bible. Some girls want to be accepted and loved so bad that they will trap a boy into a relationship by getting pregnant.

I counseled one boy who was an All-American in two sports in high school and his girlfriend was a cheerleader. They thought they were ready for "love." She became pregnant, and he turned down numerous scholarships and joined the service. He wanted to do the honorable thing and become a father and husband. But her mother talked her out of marriage, thus ruining the young man's opportunity to pursue collegiate sports. He spent three years in the Marines, got out and became a drug addict. She is still not married and has four kids by three different men.

Premarital, meaningless sex will leave you wanting and never getting the love you crave because love was awakened before it was "done."

Once again, let's go to God in prayer. Previously, we invited Jesus to be Lord and Savior of our lives, so now we want to invite the Holy Spirit to speak in our hearts and guide us through this maze called life. Allow Him to sit on the throne of your heart and direct you, and you will remain under the shadow of the Almighty. Let's pray:

> *Father, I thank You for Your Word that says If I dwell in You I am protected. I also thank You for the gift of discernment and for revealing the motives of the enemy. I choose now to put love in the slow cooker of my heart and focus on the gift within me. Holy Spirit, I invite You to speak to my heart and point me to God's best for my life. Lord, I know that if I keep my mind stays on You, You will keep me in perfect peace. Because of You, I know how special I am and I do not need to seek the acceptance of others. I know I am loved, and I thank You, Lord, In Jesus' name, Amen.*

EIGHT

The Ghosts of Relationships Past

Do you not see and know that your bodies are members (bodily parts) of Christ (the Messiah)? Am I therefore to take the parts of Christ and make [them] parts of a prostitute? Never! Never! Or do you not know and realize that when a man joins himself to a prostitute, he becomes one body with her? The two, it is written, shall become one flesh. But the person who is united to the Lord becomes one spirit with Him. Shun immorality and all sexual looseness [flee from impurity in thought, word, or deed]. Any other sin which a man commits is one outside the body, but he who commits sexual immorality sins against his own body. Do you not know that your body is the temple (the very sanctuary) of the Holy Spirit who lives within you, whom you have received [as a gift] from God? You are not your own, you were bought for a price [purchased with a preciousness and paid for, made His own]. So then, honor God and bring glory to Him in your body (1 Corinthians 6:15-20 AMPC).

This chapter is vitally important! I want to begin this chapter by taking you on a journey. We are going to a wedding! Let's meet the bride and groom, shall we? (All the names mentioned are fictitious characters for the sole purpose of illustration.) The bride is Suethal. She is twenty-eight years old and a CPA. She graduated from Harvard and has her own accounting firm. Suethal brings home about $1.6 million a year. She has just married Dashond (Chilly D), who is a point guard in the NBA. He went in the first round of the draft last year, and his current contract is for 72.3 million bucks!

They met through a mutual friend when D needed someone to handle his finances. He took one look at her and knew she was the one. The happy couple dated for a year and decided to tie the knot.

Suethal was an A student all through school, a world-class track athlete, and most of all, a born-again Christian.

She decided at a young age to remain pure so she could give her husband the ultimate gift. During their courtship, her limit, physically, was a hug and a "peck." Dashond, on the other hand, was a "playa, playa." All through school, D was popular. He was buff, good-looking, and smart. The ladies loved D, and D loved the ladies. He had been with about 400 different women before he decided to get married. He loves Suethal dearly.

The wedding is over, and they are about to go into the bedroom and consummate their marriage. They are both nervous as Suethal comes from the bathroom with her wedding night attire on.

He sees her and takes her in his arms and kisses her, but...she doesn't kiss as well as Natasha kissed, and her lips are not as soft as velvet...like Rita's. They embrace, and she is soooo soft...but not as soft as Laticia. His wife has a nice body...but not like Wanda's. Man! Wanda was off the hook! She begins to softly caress D...but not like Jennifer. Jennifer's touch made him shiver. As he lay there with his wife, he feels good...but not as god as he felt with the Calloway sisters. Boy, they were wild!

Suethal lies in her husband's arms totally pleased and satisfied. She has never felt this way before, and it's amazing for her. She has just given her husband something that no one else has ever had...herself. Her husband, Dashond, is the greatest lover in the world to her because he is her *only* lover. Suethal has nothing or no one to compare the experience to.

Dashond, on the other hand, is pleased but not satisfied. Sex with his wife is nothing like the sex he has experienced in the past, and even though he dearly loves her, he is left hungry.

Another tool of satan is to use your past to ruin your future. Ghosts of relationships past haunted Dashond. Because he did not save himself for his wife, everything she does will be compared to his past experiences. Remember when we discussed the spiritual aspects of a physical relationship? It is serious. There is no such thing as "casual" sex because every time you have sex with someone, you are transferring spirits. You take a part of them, and they in turn take a part of you.

The divorce rate in America is now nearing 70 percent. The major reason is infidelity. Infidelity occurs when a woman or man is not satisfied sexually so they go outside the marriage to find fulfillment. Why are they not satisfied? They aren't satisfied because they are comparing their spouses to past lovers and they do not stack up.

Getting back to our story, what do you think Dashond will eventually do? I guarantee you that without God's intervention, Chilly D will creep on his wife! She gave him all of herself, but he was totally incapable of doing the same because he gave so much of himself to all those other women that there was not much left to give. Those parts of himself that he gave those women will long for a "reunion," and the battle will be fierce.

The god of this world system will tell you that its best to have sex before marriage and even to live with someone before marriage so you can be sure that you are compatible, but God calls for purity. In the Old Testament, if a woman was given in marriage and she was not a virgin, she was to be stoned to death in the doorposts of her father's house. Some people will tell you it is not cool to be a virgin. To those who say that or to those who look down on you because you want to remain pure, tell them this: "I can always be like you, but you can never be like me."

A.C. Green, one of the greatest and most consistent basketball players in the NBA, with world championship rings to prove it, gave his wife a gift unmatched by any gift anyone could give her. He gave her himself! A.C. Green was a virgin before he married. I remember how the press made fun of him when they found out he had never been with a woman although he was an NBA star.

I am sure his teammates had jokes also, but he remained pure in spite of all the drama. I am sure he was tempted many times, but he did not give in to the temptation. Jesus was a virgin all His life! He was tempted! I am sure He was because the Word of God says He was (Hebrews 4:15), but He did not sin.

Television tells you that it is foolish to save yourself for marriage. The secular music industry tells you the same thing. The songs played on the major radio stations and music videos played on the music television stations promote promiscuity and even go as far as promoting homosexuality. That is why it is important to surround yourself with positive people and influences.

The people you hang around with now are actually dictating your future! Unfortunately, there are people in the church who will lead you wrong also. Keep in mind that if it goes against the Word of God, it's not for you. The right thing is not always cool, and the cool thing is not always right, so just do the right thing and don't worry about cool.

Let's go on another journey, shall we? This time we are at *your* wedding night. The candles are lit, soft good music is playing in the background, and you and your spouse give yourselves to each other. It is the most spectacular experience you could ever imagine, and you think your spouse is the greatest lover in the history of the world. Guess what? Your spouse feels the same way because neither of you had anyone to compare this experience with. There are no ghosts of relationships past because there were no relationships! Isn't it awesome? Stay pure, and it will be.

I wish someone had written a book like this for me when I was a teen. I wish I had the opportunity that you have right now. Like I said in my introduction, hindsight is always 20/20 (ask an old person what that means...I *love* those old sayings). There are things I would re-do if I had the opportunity, but I don't, so the best thing I can do is warn you of the dangers that lie ahead on the road of life. Premarital sex is one of those dangers.

Please don't go down that road. If you do, you will compare your future spouse to everyone and everything you ever experienced, and that is not fair to your future spouse.

Don't buy the lie and experiment with sex before marriage. There are too many ramifications from it.

Go back and re-read this section. It's important! Then ask God to help you stay focused on Him. He will help if you ask. Let's pray:

Father, I thank You for Your Word. It is a lamp to my feet and a light to my path. Everything that pertains to life is found in Your Word, including what You expect in marriage and the importance of sexual purity. I choose to live my life according to Your Word. I choose, today, to abstain from sexual immorality, and I am thankful that the Holy Spirit will help me to do so. Lord, I surrender my desires to You. In Jesus' name I pray, Amen.

NINE

Adam & Eve... Adam & Steve—What's the Difference?

So God let these people go their own way. They did what they wanted to do, and their filthy thoughts made them do shameful things with their bodies. They gave up the truth about God for a lie, and they worshipped God's creation instead of God, who will be praised forever. Amen. God let them follow their own evil desires. Women no longer wanted to have sex in a natural way, and they did things with each other that were not natural. Men behaved in the same way. They stopped wanting to have sex with women and had strong desires for sex with other men. They did shameful things with each other, and what has happened to them is punishment for their foolish deeds (Romans 1:24-27 CEV).

In view of the current Supreme Court decision legalizing same-sex marriages nationwide, I was led to remind you of something very important. The United States of America is not a Christian nation. This is a nation that has Christians in it. God gave us a gift called "free will," and He does not supersede our decisions. Remember also, the Word of God says, "Where sin abounded, *grace* did much more abound" (Romans 5:20 KJV, emphasis added).

There is a tale about a scorpion and a frog. The scorpion wanted to get across a pond and asked a frog for a ride. The frog was willing but asked the scorpion not to sting him. The scorpion assured the frog that he would not sting him because the frog was nice enough to help him. As they neared the other side of the pond, the frog felt this excruciating pain in his back and he said to the scorpion, "I helped you across the pond, and you told me you would not sting me but you did. Why did you go against your word?"

The scorpion stated something very profound. He said "I am grateful for your help, and I did not *want* to sting you...but it's in my nature and I had to do what I am made to do."

Sex is beautiful but only in its proper context. The God-ordained context for sex is between a married man and woman. Anything else is sin.

So much has happened in the news and throughout our nation concerning same-sex marriages and the civil rights of homosexuals (male with male and female with female). Let's deal with the civil rights portion of this argument first. A person who is Hispanic, white, Japanese, or African has no choice about the race they are born. When that child comes into this world, they are born the color and nationality of their natural parents. A black woman will not have a Chinese baby unless there is Chinese in her or the father's bloodline. The child is black and has no choice about it.

The civil rights movement was birthed to assure that everyone would be treated equally. The Civil Rights Act of 1964 was for equality for all races, colors, religions, and national origins.

Today, people can change almost everything about themselves. If you are too big, liposuction is the answer. A person can do many things to change their exterior and succeed to an extent. If you are dark and want to be light, there is something for that. If you are born Muslim and want to change your religion, you can. Nowadays a person does not have to be anything they do not want to be. As far as sexual orientation is concerned, it's no different.

Being gay is *not* a civil right. Homosexuality is a choice just like bestiality is a choice! This world system is so perverted I would not be surprised if some group arises that want civil rights for those who practice bestiality!

God created you special. He made you what you are for a specific purpose and this specific time in history. When you were born, the doctor said to your natural parent, "You have a nice bouncing baby boy or graceful baby girl." The doctor did *not* say, "Well, here ya go, mom, you have a nice healthy homosexual" or "a sweet and swinging bisexual here!"

There are rare occasions where a child is born with both sex organs (*intersexual* is the politically correct terminology) and an in-depth decision has to be made, but even in those situations, there is usually more of one reproductive system than the other. The fact of the matter is this: no one is "born gay"! Just like no one is born a whore or a backbiter and no one is born a murderer.

There are arguments that homosexuals are homosexual because they are "born that way." They cannot help it, and if they had their choice, they would not put up with the stigma and heartache of their sexual orientation. That is *true* to an extent! How? I am glad you asked!

We are born into sin, and sin has many faces. One of the many faces of sin is homosexuality. Depending upon the environment, anyone is prone to any of the many faces of sin, but sin is a choice! Homosexuals *choose* that face of sin just like a murderer chooses that particular face of sin. What this world system is trying to do is tell you, "It's alright...you were born that way." If that is the case, the murderer should not go to jail and be punished because (s)he was "born" that way.

Remember in chapter one, I told you there was nothing new under the sun? Paul was dealing with homosexuality back in his day, and we are dealing with it now. The difference is Paul did not have MTV Awards, Source Awards, BET, soap operas, governors, legislators and other venues to flaunt that face of sin. Young people think it's okay because they see their parents do it and people "coming out of the closet" on national TV. It's good that sin is coming out of the closet, but the closet needs to be *cleaned* and the person does too.

That's just another way that satan perverts the Word of God. The Word says we are to confess our sins. The world system wants us not only to confess our sins but flaunt those sins in the face of everyone like a trophy. The only way God can forgive the faces of sin we wear is present them to Him as a sacrifice of our flesh.

I am a living witness that it *hurts* to give up something you really enjoy.

I have said it before, sin is fun and good to the flesh, but in order to receive God's best for your life and the lives of those around you, you must sacrifice that "fun." In exchange, the Lord will give you a joy unspeakable.

You might say, "What do you mean I would receive God's best for me and those around me?" You have to understand the concept that your salvation is *not* just about you but also those who are to be influenced by the gift within you. You are an intricate part of the body of Christ, and others are depending on the gift in you to get the nourishment to their part of the body. The Word says God gives the increase, but someone has to plant and someone has to water. God wants that face of sin revealed and deliverance to come so others will see it can be done.

Homosexuality is what it is, a face of sin and that's it. If you are "bi-curious," Jesus is the answer to your curiosity; He says it's bad, unnatural, and a sin. He also says if you come to Him, He will deliver you from sin. He told a woman who was caught in the act of adultery (another face of sin) to "go and sin no more" (John 8:11). When he told her to "sin no more," he gave her authority over that sin in her life.

If you are battling with your sexual orientation, God wants to help you right now. What your flesh is attempting to dictate to you is real! You do "feel" different. You "desire" what's not natural to most but very natural to you. The reason it's so natural to you is because that is the face of sin that has attracted you. Now, take that face and compare it to the Word of God. He gives us a mirror to look into, and He empowers us to look into that mirror (His Word) and compare ourselves to how He really designed us. God made you, and He didn't make you gay. He made you a male with male parts to share with a female (your wife), or He made you a female with female parts to be shared with a male (your husband)!

God said he "knew" you before you were formed in your mother's womb. He knew you because He is the designer! He was the one who formed you in your mother's womb, so He knows all about you. He knew what face of sin you were prone to, and He is constantly giving you a way of escape.

Surrender that face of sin to God, and He will deliver you. Not only will He deliver you but He will use you to deliver others struggling with that same face of sin!

There are five things you must remember when you are dealing with any face of sin that has become a stronghold in your life:

- Don't try to do it alone. Tell someone, and have someone you can be accountable to.
- Be totally honest with all involved.
- Ask for forgiveness, and believe you are forgiven by God—and forgive yourself.
- Embrace your deliverance, and rejoice in God who delivered you! Every day is a faith walk, not what your used-to-be-friends say, not what you feel or what you think. It's a faith walk!
- Live every day as a new experience in Christ—as one totally delivered. A woman does not partially deliver a baby; she delivers the whole thing, and baby, you have been delivered!

In this chapter we discussed a face of sin that is growing rapidly in our culture. Remember this, homosexuality is just another face of sin and there is deliverance from it just like any other. If this sin has grabbed you and you are battling with your sexuality, I ask that you pray with me:

Lord, I realize that the things I have been feeling are against Your purpose for creating me. I see now that I am in sin. I take this time to lay upon Your altar this sin of homosexuality. I ask that You take this flesh sacrifice and burn it. I also ask that You cleanse me so You can use me to help others. I thank You for forgiving me and cleansing me, and now I repent. In Jesus' name, Amen!

TEN

No Means NO!!

Abstain from all appearance of evil...And the very God of peace sanctify you wholly; and I pray God your whole spirit and soul and body be preserved blameless unto the coming of our Lord Jesus Christ (1 Thessalonians 5:22-23 KJV).

Here's the scenario: Alphonzo is a popular senior at the local high school. He is athletic and good-looking. All of the girls like him and would *die* for the opportunity to go out with him. He is being recruited by every college in the nation for both basketball and swimming. Audrey is known as the school "tease." She dresses somewhat provocatively and loves the attention she receives from the guys, but she's never gone "all the way."

The big dance is coming up and "Zo" decides he's going to take Audrey since he can take any girl he wants. He sees her coming down the hall and winks at her. Audrey immediately melts, grabs her best friend, Tomika, by the arm, and runs into the bathroom. She asks Tomika, “Did you see what Zo just did?” Tomika replies, “Umm hmmm, girl, you’d better get that man!”

At the end of the day, Zo sees Audrey by her locker and approaches her. He says, “How would you like to go to the dance with me this weekend? I think you’re all that, baby, and we need to be getting our groove on, feel me?”

She replies, “Yeah, I’m definitely feelin’ you, but can you handle it?”

“We’ll just have to see, won’t we?” he answers as he kisses her on the cheek and walks away.

Tomika runs to her as Zo leaves, and Audrey tells her everything as they jump around. The two girls decide to go shopping for the dance. Audrey tries on several outfits before she decides on a mini-skirt with matching sheer blouse and stiletto heels. Tomika tells her, “That outfit is bangin’, girl. I am *sure* you will keep his attention!”

Zo goes all out as he arrives at her house in a stretch limousine, wearing a nice double-breasted Armani and “Gators” on his feet. He presents Audrey’s mom with flowers and awaits Audrey’s appearance. As Audrey comes downstairs, Zo is amazed at how sexy she looks. Mom sees her and pulls her into the other room, saying, “Do you think that outfit is appropriate to wear to a party, girl?”

“Mom, this is Alphonzo! He is an All-American and an honor student. He is a perfect gentleman. Look at the flowers he gave you.”

“Okay,” Mom says, “but you be careful and don’t drop anything ‘cause you certainly can’t pick it up!”

The couple says their goodbyes and head for the limo. Once inside, he presents her with a flower and a kiss. As he kisses her, his hand finds her knee and she removes it. “Girl, you look so good tonight I just had to touch you to see if I was dreaming." They go to the dance and have a great time. All the while, Zo is getting a friendly touch here and there, and she stops him. "Girl, I'm just playing," he says as he smiles at her.

They go out to dinner, and the night is wonderful. There is a half moon and the stars are out bright. Zo has an idea. "Hey, before we go in, let's take a walk. It's nice out, and it's not too late." Audrey agrees, and they pull over and begin to walk hand-in-hand in the park. Zo goes over to a beautiful landscape, gets her a flower and puts it next to her face. "The beauty of this flower pales in comparison to you," he tells her. She smiles and they kiss. He caresses her shoulders, then her waist, then goes under her skirt. She moves his hand, and he brings her closer. He then becomes an octopus as his hands go all over her, grabbing and groping, and she pulls away.

"Zo," she says, "we need to stop!"

He says, "Baby I'm sorry, I just got a little carried away. You look so sexy and all. Look, I just want a kiss, is that alright?"

"A kiss," she says, "and that's all." He takes her in his arms and kisses her gently at first but becomes more forceful as he begins to grab her body all over. He pops a button on her blouse, and she struggles to get away but he is too strong. She begins to fight but is overcome by his strength. "Please stop,'" she says, "I don't want this."

"Yes you do, and you know it," he says. "It's time to stop teasing me. You *know* you want it! Look at how you are dressed. You wanted me from the time I looked at you, and the feeling is mutual. I have spent too much money on you today to just get a kiss." He takes her behind the bushes and forces her to have sex with him.

When it's all over, he realizes that she *didn't* want it. The tears fill her eyes as she tries to gather her torn clothes. He attempts to help her, but she clams up at his touch. She bitterly weeps as she attempts to button her torn blouse, and he gives her his jacket. "I thought you were playing hard to get," he says. "Look at how you are dressed. What am I supposed to think? Do you know who I am? Every girl in the school wants me, and they all envied you tonight because you were with me. If you didn't want to give it up, you shouldn't have dressed like that and you shouldn't tease men like you do!"

Audrey looked at him and simply said, "But I said no."

Date rape is a crime! Guys need to understand that when a girl says no, she means it. Even if she didn't mean it, act as if she did! It doesn't matter what a girl has on or doesn't have on—her body is her own. No means NO! You can be in the middle of the act itself, but if a girl says stop, be a man and *stop!*

This world system wants to say it is the woman's fault if she is raped, especially if she dresses provocatively or acts promiscuous. We homo sapiens are supposed to be the supreme beings here on earth, yet we lose our supremacy and act like animals when it comes to the one of most important things in a relationship.

The National Institute of Justice reported (October 1, 2008) that 85 to 90 percent of sexual assaults reported by college women are perpetrated by someone known to their victim, and about half happen on a date. (www.nij.gov/topics/crime/rape-sexual-violence/campus/Pages/know-attacker.aspx)

We saw earlier where Amnon raped his sister because of his lust for her. After he took her, he hated her. Rape is the ultimate act of lust, power, and greed.

I sat across from a young lady whose self-esteem had been crushed by those around her because *she* was raped. She was said to be "hot," and it was her fault because of the way she acted toward the opposite sex. Her family even said she had a lot to do with the situation because of the way she dressed. She was told it was her fault because she tempted the person who raped her.

According to the Rape, Abuse and Incest National Network (RAINN), every ninety-eight seconds, somewhere in America, someone is sexually assaulted and only six out of every 1,000 perpetrators go to jail! (www.rain.org/statistics)

In the rape case of a famous boxer, it was said that the woman went to his room at two in the morning, so what was supposed to happen but sex. Another famous basketball player had his liberty with a young lady while he was recovering from surgery. Her body was bruised, but it was supposedly consensual. No female in her right mind asks to be raped.

As I write these words, my heart aches because someone reading this has experienced this trauma. Please understand that it's not okay! Your pain is real, and it was *not* your fault it happened. The healing you need only comes from Jesus. If allowed, He can take the pain and any guilt you may feel away.

Gentlemen, respect yourself! The best thing to remember when dealing with the opposite sex is "what if?" What if someone did this to my sister or my mom? How would I feel about it? Our opening scripture says it all. *Never* put yourself in the position where your flesh can have the upper hand because your flesh loves sin. Do not put yourself in a compromising position.

Have you ever seen how they boil frogs? The person will put the frog in regular water and turn the burner on. The frog will be fine in the water, and slowly the water will get hotter and hotter without the frog even noticing. The next thing you know, the frog is boiling to death. If you start out by trying to put the frog in boiling water, it would quickly jump out!

That is how sin is. The enemy will not throw you in a situation he knows you will run from. He will start with a smile. The next thing you know it's conversation, then a call from time to time. He then baits you with a date, then holding hands. None of these are bad, but the motive behind the act is what we need to consider.

After the handholding come the kiss and the caress. The kiss on the cheek becomes a smack on the lips...then a longer kiss...then an embrace with the kiss. Next, we have caresses and groping and grinding and....

As a Christian, you take Jesus with you everywhere you go, and He is there whatever you do. Ask yourself, "Would I want to take Jesus in this situation?" If the answer is "no," you don't need to go!

As we discussed in chapter four, the time may *seem* right, but it's not. Don't sell yourself short or jeopardize your blessings to get attention. What you wear on the outside is a reflection of how you are on the inside. God loves you, and He has a plan for you. He has given you everything you need to succeed in life, and the opposite sex cannot complete you. Once again, abstain.

It is important for me to define these verses at this time. According to Strong's concordance, to "abstain from all appearance of evil" means to hold one's self off or refrain thoroughly and wholly from every fashion, view, shape or appearance of hurtful, malicious, grievous harm, wickedness, moral disease, or non-virtuous acts.

The Word then says that the God of peace will sanctify you wholly and preserve you, *but* He cannot preserve you unless you abstain! This word is for the males reading this book. The word is simple, no means NO!

In this chapter, we talked about date rape and how we should respect ourselves and the wishes of others. I pray that you never face this scenario, but if you have, males, God is a forgiving God. Ask for forgiveness from Him and from the one you hurt. Females, it was not your fault he did that to you. No matter what society says, there is no double standard in the kingdom of God, and you belong to Christ. Ask God to take away the pain and believe He can and He will.

See yourself as God sees you, and go on to do His will.

Everything that we experience in life not only makes us stronger but it also equips us to help others through it. Be prepared, you have work to do! Let's pray:

Lord, I understand that in order to abstain from all appearance of evil, I must not cater to my flesh or my senses. I ask You to help me remember Your Word when it comes to the opposite sex. Lord, remind me that where I go, You go too, and whatever I do, I subject You to the same because You live within me. I refuse to grieve You anymore, so I sacrifice my desires to You. Teach me, Holy Spirit, how to better respect myself and those around me. In Jesus' name, I pray, Amen.

PART THREE

Friend or Foe?

In this section, we will discuss the definition of true friendship and look at some biblical and present-day examples of friendship. You will learn in this section that some of those you thought were friends may have been actually robbing you of your future while some of the people you really couldn't stand sometimes have been sent to speak into your life. My prayer for you is that your eyes of discernment will be opened and you will know who is a friend and who is a foe.

ELEVEN

Trusting My Parents—Why?

Children, obey your parents in the Lord [as His representatives], for this is just and right. Honor (esteem and value as precious) your father and your mother—this is the first commandment with a promise—that all may be well with you and you may live long on the earth (Ephesians 6:1-3 AMPC).

If you look at the commandment mentioned in the above verses, Exodus 20:12, you will notice that a promise is connected with the commandment. God promises you long life on the earth if you honor your father and mother. Society tells you to be mischievous and some shows on television promote outright rebellion, but that is not the way to life and true happiness.

As a counselor, an educator, and a youth pastor, I have heard them all. "Those folks are so old-fashioned...they do not understand where I am coming from." "Pressures today are far different than the pressures my parents faced back in the day." "She can't tell me to be in at a certain hour when she comes in in the wee hours of the night." "How can they tell me not to cuss, drink, and smoke when they do it all?" "How can I respect her when she doesn't even respect herself?" "Well, preacher, that's easy for you to say, you have a father or at least you know who or where your father is." "Who is he to tell me what to do when he can't even hold a job?!" "She can't tell me anything about relationships when she bounces from man to man! I can't believe how many 'uncles' I have." "How can I honor and respect a man who beats my mom like that, and how can I respect her when she allows him to do it?" "Why in the *world* should I respect someone who is a crackhead?" "But he touched me in places he shouldn't have." "What is there to honor, what is there to respect?"

The first thing you must remember is your parents had the option to let you live or die. Yes, it was God's plan for you to live, but God can only work through a willing vessel. He will not override a person's will, and if your parents had chosen to abort you, you would not be here today. Yes, they would have been out of the will of God and your blood would have been on their hands, but they had a choice and they chose to listen to God and bring you, another of God's miracles, to the earth. This is a reason to honor your parents.

Second, you may be an adopted child and not know who your real parents are. You may be in search of your identity and feel abandoned. *Don't!* God loves you so much He brought you forth even though your natural parents were not ready. Your natural parents were merely an avenue used by God to get you here.

Go back to chapter two and reflect on how wonderful you really are and how He formed you, called you, appointed you, and anointed you! You were sent to earth for such a time as this. Your assignment was so vital that He gave you a family, and the family He gave you is the one you need. The fact of the matter is they need you too!

I understand the pain you may feel being in an abusive environment, and it hurts me and God to know it's being done. The abuse stems form a lack of self-respect. If a person does not respect their own self, they will not respect anyone else. The majority of the time they will take their frustrations out on someone weaker. This kind of activity can only be stopped through legal intervention and prayer.

So how do you honor an abusive parent? Pray for them, and when you pray, do like Jesus. Even though Lazarus was dead four days (John 11:17) and the little girl was also dead (Mark 5:39-42), Jesus spoke *life* to them. Pray for your parents! Honor them by praying for them. When you see them doing things that aren't pleasing to the Lord, give those things to Him! Speak positively and call those things that are not as though they are.

Parents aren't perfect, and if you are the first child or the only child, you are "the great experiment"! It does not matter how many books a parent reads or how many brothers and sisters your parents have. The first child is new to them, and they don't know what to do. Each day is a challenge, and they also have to learn how to get past "self" to raise another human being. Even if you have other brothers and sisters younger or older, your parents still aren't perfect.

God may have also put you in a family of unbelievers. You are there for a reason. Seek God's face, and find out how you can be an effective witness to those in your family.

The Word of God says, "Your sons and daughters will prophesy" (Acts 2:17). God does not make mistakes; you are hooked up with your family for a reason. Allow God to use you the way He wants to in your family. You can learn from the mistakes of your parents and from the victories. Observe them and apply the positive to your life. Honor your parents, and thank God for them.

In Ephesians 6, God said you would be rewarded with long life. As I read that scripture, the Lord took me back to the time I worked at a juvenile detention center (youth prison). When you walked on the property, you could feel the presence of doom. Those kids were morbid. Most of them would spend the rest of their lives in and out of prison. They were the walking dead. Why? They refused to listen to the counsel of their parent or parents. They listened to "Jonadab" when he told them how they could become popular or how they could fit in, and they went straight to prison. They did not have long life because in prison there is only death.

Think also about the young people around you whose lives have been cut short in various ways.

Your parents are there to help you succeed. They teach you right from wrong by word and example. Some examples may not be the examples you expect, but they are still examples. By honoring the lessons you learn from them, you will became a better person and you will ultimately be around to teach others.

I said previously that you have both natural and spiritual parents. You must honor your spiritual parents also. I was blessed with spiritual parents who loved me so much they stayed on me.

They would not get off my back, and I am thankful. I had two spiritual guides (yes I was blessed) who spoke into my life. They were both pillars of the community, had wonderful ministries, and were well versed in the Word.

Both made me do things I did not want to do, and when one would spank me, I would run to the other and I would get a spanking there too! They both saw something special in me and would not give up on me even when I gave up on myself. I thank God for these two men, Dr. Sam Davis and the Late Bishop George D. Lee III, who taught me the Word by example.

Dr. Davis made me help conduct a funeral right after my father transitioned. It was the hardest thing I had done, but I knew I could do anything after I did it. He saw my potential and knew me well enough to push me beyond my natural boundaries.

Bishop Lee would not let me wallow in self-pity after failing again and again. Instead he told me "Get up boy, wipe your knees, and get your tail back to work!" Your spiritual parents deserve honor, and long life is guaranteed to you if you honor them.

My natural parents were a hoot! My mama told it like it was and cut no corners doing it. She loved her children and would protect them by any means necessary!

I remember when I was young and we lived in Germany. A woman hit me. Honey, Annie Ruth went out there and asked her why, and before the woman could respond, Annie knocked her out with one punch then she stepped over her. Her natural instinct was to protect her kids. As I previously stated, my father was an ex-drill sergeant, a golden-glove boxer, and a chef. He taught his sons how to cook as my mom taught us how to sew. My dad was hard. We had to awaken at "0600 hours" on Saturday mornings to clean the house. Our wooden floors were so clean you could eat off them, and the faucets were so shiny you could shave in them.

We were well disciplined. Yes, there were times of rebellion, but "Doc" knew how to reel us back in. Neither of my parents spared the rod, and I am grateful for it. When I was coming up, my mom worked in the elementary school I attended, so when I acted up, they simply sent me to her and I would get a "whooping" right there in the hallway.

I honored my natural parents when they were alive. I love them dearly, and I miss them. Another reason to honor them is because you never know when they will leave you. Everyone will pass to eternity, and you do not want your parents to go with unsolved problems. I am at peace because my parents and I had a loving relationship before they passed. Do your parents or parent a favor. Do yourself a favor. Stop right now, put this book down, and go tell them thanks for life and that you love them. Tell both your natural and spiritual parents. It will minister to their hearts and yours as well, and God will bless your obedience to His prompting.

Well, once again, God has opened our eyes to His Word and spoken to our hearts. In sowing that seed of honor to your parents you will reap a shower of blessings in your life.

There are times when you don't agree with your parents, but remember, they have been down that road, and even though you don't understand why, they...

- Don't want you to go there;
- Don't want you to mess with that boy;
- Don't like that "hoochie mama";
- Don't want you to be around those people, girl;
- Don't want you to do that!

Listen to what they say and obey because the Word of God says, "To obey is better than sacrifice and to hearken [to listen] than the fat of rams [to try to make up for it]. For rebellion is as the sin of witchcraft, and stubbornness is as idolatry and...[good luck images]" (1 Samuel 15:22-23 AMPC). Let's pray:

Father, I thank You for Your Word. I thank You for my parents both, natural and spiritual. Lord, even though I may not understand why I have to do certain things or why I am not allowed to do things others can do, I have faith that You will make it all work for good and I will be a better person because of obedience. I thank You in advance for long life because of my decision to live according to Your Word. This I pray in Jesus' name, Amen.

TWELVE

Godly Examples

A friend loves at all times, and a brother is born for a time of adversity (Proverbs 17:17 NIV).

In chapter one, we looked at Amnon and Jonadab. We looked at their relationship and came to the conclusion that Jonadab was not a true friend. Anytime your "friend" advises you to do something contrary to the Word of God, they do not have your best interest in mind. A true friend would not allow you to break the law, endanger yourself or someone else, lie, cheat, or go against your parents' word. Jonadab advised his younger cousin to lie to his father and his sister in order to get what he wanted. Listening to Jonadab caused shame to Amnon's family and ultimately caused Amnon to lose his life.

I mentioned my best friend, David, in chapter one. David was and still is a true friend. When we were in college, I ran track for Western Kentucky University. Sometimes, before a meet, I would get nervous. I remember calling

David in the middle of the night, and he would go down to the track with me so I could run off the nervousness. David told me the truth, and he never sugar coated it. Had it not been for David taking my gun when I wanted to shoot my enemy, I would not be writing this book now. I wouldn't be married to the most wonderful woman in the world, but instead, I would be in prison or dead for murder.

Speaking of my wife, I am blessed! My wife is the "Proverbs 31 woman." She is a true friend. As much as my wife loves me, she will *not* go against the Word of God for my sake. I once asked her to call in for me when I did not feel like going to work, and she refused! That woman told me, "Honey, I love you, but I will not lie for you." I was amazed and loved her even more. Because she would not lie *for* me, I knew she would not lie *to* me.

Look at the friends you hang with right now. What are they doing? Are their actions in line with the Word of God? People will fall into one of two categories. They are either making deposits into your life or making withdrawals from your life. If they are constantly begging for this or that and never giving, they like you for what they can get. They are like leeches sucking the life from you. A true friend will make deposits into your life and will protect your best interests.

Look at Proverbs 17:17. The Word says a friend *loves* at all times.

In 1 Corinthians 13:4-8, Paul describes what love is:

> *Love endures long and is patient and kind; love is never envious nor boils over with jealousy, is not boastful or vainglorious, does not display itself haughtily. It is not conceited (arrogant and inflated with pride); it is not rude (unmannerly), and does not act unbecomingly.*

Love (God's love in us) does not insist on its own rights or its own way, for it is not self-seeking; it is not touchy or fretful or resentful; it takes no account of the evil done to it [pays no attention to a suffered wrong]. It does not rejoice at injustice and unrighteousness, but rejoices when right and truth prevail. Love bears up under anything and everything that comes, is ever ready to believe the best of every person, its hopes are fadeless under all circumstances, and it endures everything [without weakening]. Love never fails [never fades out or becomes obsolete or comes to an end] (AMPC).

Does your friend meet the definition? Another word for a friend is an accountability partner. A true friend will keep you in check and help you achieve your goals in life. Looking through the Bible, you will find some great examples of true friendship.

Let's look at David. David and King Saul's son Jonathan were so close they were like brothers. Their souls were knit together, and Jonathan loved David as his own life. King Saul was crazy with jealousy against David, and he told his son and his servants that they must kill David, but Jonathan went to bat for his friend against a crazy man. He loved his friend so much he defended him and loved his father so much he would not let him sin and kill David.

Will your friend have your back, or will they run in the midst of your trouble?

Jesus had seventy followers He sent, twelve disciples He taught, and then He had three dear friends who He could confide in and truly trust. Those friends were Peter, James, and John. When Jesus wanted someone to really talk to, He had Peter, James, and John. They were there at the mount of transfiguration and at the garden of Gethsemane. Jesus, the Son of God, trusted them enough to tell them His problems, and He knew they would not repeat them to anyone.

Peter loved Jesus with all his heart, but when the rubber met the road, he choked under pressure. What would your friends do? Peter remembered the words he told Jesus, "Man, I got your back, and I am down! If you go down, I am going down with you!"

What did Peter do? He denied Jesus. Afterwards, he was so crushed that he hurt his friend, he wept bitterly.

Jesus' love for Peter was so strong that He forgave him. Jesus did not tell Peter, "Man, I thought you had my back" or "See, I told you you were weak." He never mentioned the wrong done, He simply told him, "Feed my sheep." What did Jesus mean by that statement? It was a gesture of His forgiveness and the restoration of their relationship.

Afterwards, when the Holy Spirit came, it was Peter, the close friend of Jesus and the man Jesus knew He could trust with His Word, who preached the first sermon. Even after Peter had denied Jesus three times, Jesus blessed him.

Have you ever had a friend that crossed you? What did you do? Are there still ill feelings toward that friend? If so, forgive them *now!* Go to that friend and tell them if you can. If they are not dead, make an effort to talk to them and apologize. "But Pastor Holmes, you don't know what they did to me or what they said about me." It doesn't matter! Release them for your sake! If you don't release them, they become a god in your life! What do I mean? Glad you asked! Think about it.

When you are angry at or have a grudge against someone, every time you see or even think about him or her, your day is ruined. You think about what they did and get mad.

That is exactly what satan wants you to do! That person becomes a form of worship because they change you from "glory to Gory."

Everything is fine until they come to mind. That anger starts out small, but as time goes on, it grows and grows until your mind is consumed with how you were done wrong by that person. You can see that person at church and you suddenly do not feel like worshipping God anymore because the god of unforgiveness has taken the throne of your life and heart. That is why it is vitally important to squash it! Do not let unforgiveness block your blessings. God cannot forgive you if you have not forgiven others (Mark 11:25-26).

When you approach that person, it is best not to point fingers. Someone has to be the big person, so why not let it be you? Even though you were not wrong in the situation, you were wrong by not forgiving.

I recall once when Annette and I had a disagreement. I was obviously in the right, but I know her. Going to her and telling her how wrong she was would have made things worse, so I asked God what to do. He said, "Apologize to her for harboring animosity toward her and walking in sin." This opened the door for us to openly communicate about the situation, never pointing the finger at the other.

I have given you some godly examples of true friendship and how to maintain and restore a friendship. Good friends are rare. People have many associates but very few friends. Jesus had seventy in the outer circle, He had twelve in the inner circle, but He only had three intimate friends.

Find someone to motivate you and who you can be accountable to. Make sure they love the Lord and earnestly want to serve Him, and you will have a "Jonathan" in your corner. Let's go to God in prayer:

Lord, I thank You for giving me godly examples of true friendship. I also thank You for reminding me just how harmful unforgiveness can be. Holy Spirit, I invite You to show me my true friends and help me to let go of those who don't have my best interest at heart. Help me to trust my natural and spiritual parents' judgment in the area of friendships, and help me to make godly decisions and not just the "popular" ones. This I pray in Jesus' name, Amen.

THIRTEEN

Finding Myself

I have hidden your word in my heart that I might not sin against you (Psalm 119:11 NIV).

The Word of God contains everything we need to be successful in life. The answer to every question is there. Examples of how to fail and succeed are there. All you need is the faith of a child. I look at my son and see exactly what God's Word means. Daniel II totally believes beyond a shadow of a doubt that I will take care of him. He does not get out on the street and beg for food because he knows his daddy will feed him. He does not have a job but stays well-dressed because he knows his daddy will clothe him. Not only does little Daniel know that I will take care of his needs, but he comes to me in confidence that his desires will be granted as long as he does what he is supposed to do. If he does what Daddy requires of him, he can ask Daddy for anything and get it.

That is exactly how our heavenly Father is. He wants to bless us. He wants us to prosper in every avenue of our lives, but

He can't bless our mess. He said if we are willing and obedient, we will eat the good of the land (Isaiah 1:19). Just as I have requirements for little Daniel, God has requirements for me.

I chose this chapter to deal with an assortment of issues, from sexual desires to music, so buckle your seatbelt and let's go!

Sex

We went over why you should not even stress over the issue of sex, and I discussed something that is becoming more prevalent today than ever before. Homosexuality is a sin. God ordained marriage but not same-sex marriage. He said in His Word, "For this reason a *man* shall leave his father and his mother, and be joined to his *wife*; and they shall become one flesh" (Genesis 2:24 AMPC, emphasis added). It was a sin in the Old Testament, a sin in the New Testament, and a sin today! There is no gray area in this issue. Man was created for woman, and woman was created for man. If that were not the case, God would have created us asexual. Please read the instructor's manual and you will see for yourself. Here are a few scriptures to point you in the right direction:

- Leviticus 18:22
- 1 Corinthians 6:9-10
- Genesis 19:4-9
- Romans 1:24-32

What I would suggest is that you read those scriptures in several different translations of the Bible in order to get the picture.

Music

Yes, I have to go there. I have always been in love with music. When I was not a Christian, I worked at a radio station and I had a show called "Music for Lovers" from midnight until 3:00 a.m.

When I became a Christian, I threw all of my secular music away! I told the Lord that He created me to *love* music, so He would have to turn me on to some good Christian music. I researched and found out that the world has nothing on the kingdom of God when it comes to music! God opened the door for me to become a Christian music director at a radio station for six years, and I learned how varied Christian music is.

If you like rap music, God has some Christian rap artists that are off the hook! While I am there, let me tell you why rap is so important in the kingdom of God. Rap music has aggressive beats and lyrics both in the secular realm and in the realm of the Spirit. The difference is secular rap is basically destructive in the natural. It degrades women, glorifies murder and gang violence, and promotes drug use and antisocial behaviors.

Christian rap music damages the kingdom of darkness. It penetrates satan's domain and runs demons out! It talks about defeating the enemy and stepping on his head. It talks about being mighty in the Spirit and putting on the armor of God.

Christian rock is just as aggressive in its praise. I pray that you sit down with your parents and share some good Christian music with them. There is Christian music for every type of music lover, and all of it is anointed. Go to your local Christian music store and ask for the type of music you like. God has it! He created music, and satan perverted it. Don't go for substitutes...get the original!

Clothes

This one is simple. The Word of God says in Romans 12:2 (NIV), "Do not conform any longer to the patterns of this world but be transformed by the renewing of your mind." The bottom line is if people cannot see the Spirit of God in you because of what is "on" you, something is wrong. Unfortunately, man looks on the outward appearance, so it would be difficult for me to focus on your message if you come to me wearing a miniskirt and a sheer blouse. I am not saying that you must cover everything from your neck to your toes; I am saying honor your parents (natural and spiritual) and ask yourself one question, "Would Jesus wear this?"

Drugs

I guarantee you there is no greater high than the infilling of the Holy Spirit. To tangibly feel the presence of the Lord is *awesome*. Let's conduct an experiment right now.

If there is someone near you, within the sound of your voice, call his or her name. What happened? I bet they answered you by either saying huh, what, yeah or something to that effect. If they didn't verbally answer you, they came to you, right? That is exactly what our Lord and Savior does. He said He would be with us, "all the days (perpetually, uniformly, and on every occasion) to the [very] close and consummation of the age" (Matthew 28:20 AMPC). When you earnestly call the name of Jesus, He answers! Guess what? If you don't think He will answer...He won't.

He cannot answer to your fear; He can only respond to your faith. When Jesus answers you, you are filled with His presence and the "buzz" comes. With a Jesus buzz, there is no hangover!

Did you think the person you called during our experiment above would answer you? So you had *faith* they would. Have the same kind of faith that the Lord will answer you, and He will.

Drugs are an imitation or perversion of the high you get when you are in the presence of the Lord. When the Holy Spirit came on the day of Pentecost, some people thought the saints were "drunk and full of sweet [intoxicating] wine" (Acts 2:13 AMPC).

But Peter set them straight. He told them,

> *For these men are not drunk, as you imagine, for it is [only] the third hour (about 9:00 a.m.) of the day; But [instead] this is [the beginning of] what was spoken through the prophet Joel: And it shall come to pass in the last days, God declares, that I will pour out of My Spirit upon all mankind* (Acts 2:15-17 AMPC).

Why get drunk on a substitute? You may as well have the real thing! The high the world offers will make you see monsters and do illegal things to get more. It will make you want to kill yourself or someone else. The high the Lord gives you will allow you to speak into someone's life, lay hands on the sick, and raise the dead. God's high will allow you to cast out demons and speak words of healing to the sick in heart. It's your choice. Which buzz do you want to get?

The last question I want to pose to you is this. Who is in charge of your life? When you go into outer space, what do you wear? You wear a spacesuit. When you go scuba diving, what do you wear? You wear a scuba suit, right? These are suits that you wear to be able to function in a particular environment. God said He made us in His image, and God is Spirit. If we are made in the image of God, we are also spirit. We are a spirit, we have a soul, and we live in a body. This body is what I call an "earth suit." We said that we use a scuba suit for the water and a space suit for space, so I submit to you we have an earth suit for the earth!

With that in mind, when an astronaut goes into space and puts on his space suit, does the suit dictate to the person inside what to do or does the person in the suit move the suit about where they please? When a diver goes underwater, who is in charge the man or the suit?

How, then, can we allow our earth suits to dictate to us (the spirit inside, the *real* us) what to do and what not to do? If a space suit malfunctions, the astronaut gets another. When our flesh gets out of line, we must kill it!

Paul said in 1 Corinthians 15:31 (AMPC), "I die daily," which means "I put the flesh under subjection to the real me!"

Jesus said, "If your hand offends you, cut it off. It is better to lose one part of your body" (Mark 9:43-48). Jesus mentioned three things in those verses.

First, he mentioned the hand (verse 43), or what you do. Do the work of the Lord. He said we should work (do) while it is day. In other words, God wants us to be about His business. With all of these examples, Jesus said something astounding. He said if it offends *you,* cut it off.

Jesus then mentions the foot (verse 45), or where you go. My great aunt Madeline Saunders had a wonderful word of encouragement to those who left her presence. She would always say, "Take Jesus with you." That is a profound statement! In other words, Aunt Madeline was saying if you cannot take Jesus where you're going, you don't need to go there. Jesus said if where you go is causing you to sin..."cut it off!"

Finally, He mentioned the eye (verse 47), or what you see. Don't feed on things that are not spiritually uplifting. The internet is another of satan's great tools today. While you have to be eighteen to go and buy an adult magazine, anyone can access the net. Do not poison your spirit with pornography. Porn can also be a "ghost of relationships past" if you have an intimate relationship with pornography. Job said, "I made a covenant with my eyes not to look lustfully at a young woman...does he not see my ways and count my every step?" (Job 31:1-4 NIV). Jesus said if it offends you, gouge it out!

What you must do is put your earth suit in check if it tries to take over. It's up to you to remind your earth suit who is in charge.

There is no secret to life. Life is most enjoyed when you discover your gift and share it with the world. Proverbs 3:5-6 wraps it all up in a nice package, "Trust in the LORD with all your heart and lean not on your own understanding. In all your ways submit to him, and he will make your paths straight" (NIV).

But What If...

Because Jesus is the only perfect person to walk the face of the earth, we will sometimes miss the mark. The Word of God says, "all have sinned and fall short of the glory of God" (Romans 3:23 NIV). When we *do* sin, satan comes in and condemns us for what we have done. We feel there is no hope for us, and we go deeper and deeper in sin because we listen to the lie that God will not forgive us. There is nothing you can do that is so bad that God will not forgive you except not respecting and listening to the Holy Spirit and accepting Christ as Lord and Savior. There is no way I can condone sin. God does not condone sin, but God does love the sinner. He wants you to come to Him. He wants to bless you, but His blessings are conditional and He cannot bless your sin.

What do I mean? Remember the analogy I gave you about being under God's umbrella of protection? If you decide to get out from under the umbrella, God will not make you come back. As much as He wants to keep you from getting wet with sin, He gave you a will and He will not go against your will. As soon as you decide to get back under the umbrella, He is there with open arms to receive you. Let's say, for instance, you missed the mark in some way. God's Word says if you confess your sin, He is faithful and just to forgive your sins and cleanse you from all unrighteousness (1 John 1:9).

What is sin? Sin, in a nutshell, is allowing your earth suit to dictate to the real you how to act and react. When this happens, satan, the accuser, comes in and makes you feel totally defeated. You will feel like God is miles away from you when He is actually right there just waiting for you to say the word. He wants to give you the royal ring and robe, but He can't until you come to Him.

Once you ask God to forgive your sin, He will not only forgive you, but He will restore you.

Repenting means to turn around and go in the opposite direction. Remember the two roads I mentioned in chapter one? When you repent, you simply come to the realization that you are on the wrong road and you turn around to get on the right one. If you have missed the mark in any way, in any area of your life, God will forgive you if you simply come to Him and ask. Not only will He forgive you, God will totally forget about your sin. His Word says, "as far as the east is from the west, so far has He removed our transgressions from us" (Psalm 103:12 AMPC).

Once God has forgiven you, you need to forgive yourself. The thing satan will do is remind you of your past so you will miss the blessings ahead that God has for you. Don't let "self unforgiveness" stop you from walking in the very best God has for you.

Our destiny is not revealed in tarot cards, the zodiac, or "Polly Palm-Reader." It's not found in the tel-"lie"-vision shows the world offers, or in the music that satan has perverted. It's not in the movie stars or the multi-million dollar athletes. If you really look at their lives you will see some of the unhappiest, superficial rich people in the world. Once again, money cannot buy joy or inner peace. It's all in the Word of God. Go to the Word and discover your royal heritage.

Finding yourself begins with the fear of the Lord. Society will tell you "do what you feel," but God sent me to tell you, "Don't buy the lie!" Let's pray:

Lord, I thank You for Your Word that tells me You want me to prosper and be in health even as I gain knowledge. I understand that I am in charge of this "earth suit," and You empowered me to keep it in line. I make a covenant with You now that I will apply what I learned in this book to my everyday life. By doing this, You will be pleased and I will walk in victory. In Jesus' name, I pray, Amen.

About the Author

Daniel Solomon Holmes currently serves as the Chief Executive Officer (CEO) and President of Relationship Builders, LLC located in Richmond, Virginia. He formerly served as the Pastor of Shalom Ministries, Inc., a ministry of restoration and reconciliation established in Augusta, Georgia. He is actively serving in the Intercessory Prayer Ministry, and as a Team Leader of the Marriage Ministry and the Ministerial Staff at Mt. Gilead Full Gospel International Ministries in Richmond, VA. He is a well sought-after motivational speaker and teacher at conferences, retreats and within the school and university systems. Pastor Holmes is a licensed educator, certified mental health professional, dedicated track & field coach, and an Executive Board member for Special Olympics (Urban Programs) in the Richmond, VA area. He also serves as a sponsor for the Fellowship of Christian Athletes (FCA). Daniel and his wife, Annette, have been married for 34 years and have been mentoring married couples for over thirty years. The have two delightful children, Shekinah Joye and Daniel Solomon II. They currently reside in Midlothian, VA.

CPSIA information can be obtained
at www.ICGtesting.com
Printed in the USA
BVOW09s0809281117
501340BV00007B/126/P

9 781460 009048